the Survival Bible for Women in Medicine

In appreciation to
H. Richard Winn, MD
Professor, Surgeon and Mentor

the Survival Bible for Women in Medicine

Kathryn Ko, M.D.

Associate Professor, Division of Neurosurgery,
Robert Wood Johnson University of Medicine & Dentistry,
New Jersey

The Parthenon Publishing Group

International Publishers in Medicine, Science & Technology

NEW YORK   LONDON

Published in the USA by
The Parthenon Publishing Group Inc.
One Blue Hill Plaza
PO Box 1564, Pearl River
New York 10965, USA

Published in the UK and Europe by
The Parthenon Publishing Group Limited
Casterton Hall, Carnforth
Lancs. LA6 2LA, UK

Library of Congress Cataloging-in-Publication Data
Ko, Kathryn
    The survival bible for women in medicine / Kathryn Ko.
        p.   cm.
    ISBN 1-85070-752-9
    1. Women in medicine. 2. Women physicians—Vocational guidance.
I. Title
    [DNLM: 1. Internship and Residency. 2. Vocational Guidance.
3. Women.   W 20 K75s 1997]
R692.K6 1997
610.69′52′082—dc21
DNLM/DLC
for Library of Congress   97-15485
                                                                CIP

British Library Cataloguing in Publication Data
Ko, Kathryn
    The survival bible for women in medicine
    1. Women in medicine 2. Women physicians – Life skills guides
  . I. Title
    610.6′9′082

ISBN 1-85070-752-9

Typeset by Martin Lister Publishing Services, Carnforth, UK
Printed in the USA

Contents

Foreword

I am a part of the feminization of American medicine, a minuscule player in the changing landscape of a profession whose pulse, until recently, was transfixed by men with women in supporting roles at home, in the office and in the hospital. This type of organization allowed men to focus their efforts single-mindedly on medicine and to build this great field into what it is today. We have inherited a profession whose lifestyle is difficult to reconcile with the basic definition of what it is to be a woman. Women are therefore unlikely to travel the road that many of the men took because the steps they left for us are too narrow for all the roles we live. The medical profession may eventually evolve to accommodate our needs and our biology but until then it is up to women to create the means to build careers and lives that bring satisfaction. I have found the following information useful toward achieving personal and professional balance and I bequeath this book, my small contribution, to all those women who in my specialty I have not yet seen to mentor. May your journey be if not a little shorter at least a little kinder.

1   Preparation

Balance

With medical school begins the first step in the long odyssey to become a doctor. Along with the choice of a medical career comes a lifestyle that by virtue of its unpredictability can be professionally self-centered. Pause a moment and ask what you want from life? What is important to you in addition to your career? Medical school is the time to consider these questions in order to plan residency and practice within the confines of what will make you as a woman fulfilled. When you understand what you need to become whole, only then can you work towards a complementary personal and professional life. You will have to fight hard to balance these aspects, so start now. Biomedical education will take care of the academics, you must take care of yourself and find the means to grow personally during the many years spent on the path to becoming a physician.

The usual progression from college to medical school through residency and finally onto practice has the approval stamp of tradition on it. Although this is the approach that medical education has supported for decades, you don't have to go from one entity to the next immediately. Just because it works for a lot of people, if it doesn't suit you, step off the track for a while.

Don't be shy about taking time off to do research, have a baby, or fulfil any other personal dream. Having the courage to take a side road could open up even greater career doors than if you had stayed on the typical track and you will be happier for having followed it. Remember a woman's career need not unfold within the same time frame as a man's.

I did a two year basic science research fellowship after internship and before residency. Because it was a day job with no call, I traveled, learned the computer, attended concerts, caught up on reading, enjoyed the company of family and friends and barely touched a medical journal during this time. Even though this involved a cross country relocation, it was a precious period of breath-catching and exploration that removed me from direct involvement in the clinical scene. I am grateful for that laboratory experience because it taught me to problem-solve both mechanically and intellectually, and, in addition, it helped my career immensely. That time also allowed me to ponder basic questions and implement strategy for residency and for life.

Getting in the door

The time to start planning for residency is really the day medical school begins. Geographical considerations and career goals hark back to the idea of knowing what you want to do with life and career, where and with whom? If you plan to have a family in the future, start investigating this now since having a child is one of the greatest challenges women face in medical school and residency because of the rigidity inherent in these programs. As you clarify the non-medical needs and goals you will select an area of medicine to call your own. While working within the framework of these personal parameters, shoot for the best residency program. This will serve you well later and afford a stronger bargaining position throughout your career. Where you trained in residency is more important to other medical professionals than where you went to medical school, a question most commonly asked by nonmedical persons.

The techniques needed to get selected for residency are similar to those used in applying for medical practice positions. The same interview techniques, requests for letters of recommendation and curriculum vitae preparation apply. So take an interest in learning about this process and perfecting your approach, as this will be repeated in the future. Remember that in applying for residency or any job, a supportive phone call to a potential employer from a respected person who knows your work is worth a hundred reference letters. This is not something you can ask a person to do, but hint like hell about it to get them on the phone. Build a gallery of supporters and nurture these relationships since you will need letters and advisors throughout your career. If introduced to someone in your field who shows an interest in you, initiate a correspondence. Remaining in touch by letters or e-mail will keep your name in their minds. Every time an award is won, a presentation is made, an article is published or anything of note accomplished, keep them informed of this progress. When requesting written recommendations, ask these people to send a copy of the letter to you and to keep one permanently in their files.

> *My undergraduate biochemistry professor, who I have known almost 20 years, still writes my letters of recommendation and issues words of advice as needed.*

Getting to know those who make key decisions personally is beneficial because they are more likely to give you a job if they know you. Introduce yourself to the chairpersons of departments that you are considering for residency. Even if you do not take a job at that particular institute, you can still gain a strong letter of recommendation from that person which will carry political clout.

Curriculum vitae

Examine other people's curriculum vitaes including those of professors, to decide the best way to design yours. Limit your CV to one page followed by a list of publications or presentations or anything that distinguishes you from the hungry pack. Have a trusted faculty member review the CV for final approval on the contents and format. Continually update and refine the CV to reflect new changes. Store the CV on a word processor for easy updating and prepare a professional-looking document with a laser printer.

Interview

A job can be won or lost in the span of a 20 minute conversation. Schedule several practice interviews with staff members at school before the real one. Look professional; wear a conservative neat suit, not slacks. Never arrive more than 5 minutes early and don't be late, but if it happens, call. Walk into the interview and identify yourself with your hand held out to shake. Men normally shake hands when meeting and leaving, so do the same. Avoid wasting substantial time on pleasantries, you have limited time to sell yourself. If you want that job tell them why they need you and make these points early. Don't assume they remember your accomplishments detailed on the CV. Reiterate these in person by repeating what's on the CV and emphasizing the highlights. Don't be shy about bragging, men do it all the time.

Do pre-interview homework by looking up your interviewers in the *Index Medicus* to inspect their latest publications and become familiar with areas of their biomedical expertise. Think up reasonable questions that sincerely convey an interest in their accomplishments ahead of time. Have a few questions ready regarding the institute as they invariably ask 'Now what questions do you have about this program?'

Prepare answers ahead of time to personal questions regarding marriage, children, and family. If asked about pregnancy or children, put the question back in their court and inquire what their experience has been with previous women in the program and how this was handled. This will enlighten you about their exposure to this issue and whether or not this is even considered feasible to them. Reassure them that if you do get pregnant it is your intention to cooperate fully with the 'team' in maintaining the smooth running of their service and that you will be committed toward a solution if such a situation arises.

Redirect the conversation and reinforce your dedication to medicine, academic pursuits and their program. Send a brief thank-you note to those who interviewed you and mention positive aspects of the visit. Maintain a professional demeanor because even if you don't get this job there may be an opportunity in the future at that institute – it happened to me. Also use the interview period during the fourth year to sightsee and explore the cities visited. Get in the habit early of combining personal growth with career advancement.

Talk the talk

After the interview speak to the residents about the day-to-day nitty-gritty, number of calls, back up, what it's really like, etc. Get an idea of the rotations and the structure of the program. A discussion with the *least* senior resident will often reveal the most accurate assessment of the day-to-day operations. Find out what books are a must to purchase and which pocket guides are indispensable to carry around in the white coat. Inquire about the required journal subscriptions. Ask the women their opinions on how they have been treated in general, and specifically about pregnancy. Find out if there are any personal safety issues.

Write your impressions down in a residency file. Gain something from each interview and rate your own performance. Persuasive interview techniques and interpersonal skills are useful when dealing with patients in a competitive medical practice. These one-on-one exchanges turn out to be the life blood of medicine. Learn to be as polished in these up-close conversations as you are in front of an audience.

Match

The time to start organizing for residency is Match Day. I had to move 6000 miles for my residency so if this involves physically moving to another city for you, plan the move well ahead of July 1st. I suggest moving to the new location at least 2 weeks prior to starting. Cardboard boxes should be used for moving and are easy to get in any hospital central supply room. Do as much of the move prep by phone during the remaining months of the fourth year. Call the residency staff office and request assistance with housing. Hospital housing is actually set up for the life of a resident. The housing is usually located near the hospital with all the amenities on site. I lived in hospital housing for 6 years and with my erratic hours it was the *safest* housing I could afford at that time. Get the actual apartment number and start forwarding the mail and journal subscriptions early. Arrange to have all utilities up and operational prior to July 1st. The 4th of July weekend is particularly busy and you could be spending the first holiday of residency in the hospital on call.

No match

If committed to a specific residency but did not match, assess your chances. Maybe another field will do, maybe the CV needs a boost through research and publications, further schooling (PhD) or maybe you need the right 'connections'. I recommend at least one clinical year after medical school so that you are eligible for a state medical license. If you have still not succeeded in obtaining your residency of choice one option is to arrange a research fellowship in which the duties are limited to the laboratory thereby affording the time to engage in basic science work. This can help boost the chances of getting into a competitive residency, other fellowship or an academic position. A research fellowship at a prestigious institute can be easier to get than a selective residency at that same facility. Often academic clinical chairpersons who maintain research laboratories may reject the residency application but hire you for a research position. After having performed well in the laboratory you have increased the probability of being offered a residency spot, if not in their program, then elsewhere and you've gained a prominent backer in your court. Go to the most prestigious lab possible within your personal framework. Make certain that you are included as an author on any publication to which your work contributed. Adding publications will enhance your CV and make you more marketable whatever your career becomes.

Be aware that there are also salaried nonresidency positions at certain programs that allow you to function in the capacity of a resident with the possibility that after a year of devotion you may be admitted to the program as one. This is risky and you may not get residency credit for the year, but if lucky you can get into a competitive specialty through this route. At the very least you will have gained clinical experience in a field that you may enter.

Medical school to residency marks an important transition phase in the maturation of a doctor. The responsibility magnifies and there will be additional stresses as the role of doctor becomes real. The following chapter will guide you through this transition. Keep in mind that the goal is to complete a residency but not surrender the best years of young adult life to it. Save some time for yourself to do those other things that mean a lot to you. Don't postpone all other important goals until after residency, it will not be any easier later on and you will be older.

2 Operating

Try not to make residency the major focal point of existence and remember that life away from the hospital is important. If life revolves around the hospital only, you will not have the chance to evolve as a person. You will walk into residency at age 26 and leave 5 years later, older but personally not much wiser because the normal development that most young people experience during this time may have been lost in the fatigue and discipline required to complete a residency. Attend to those other dreams so that when residency is finished, you will be happier that not everything else was left behind to pursue the calling of the medical profession.

During time off in residency forget about hospital matters, there will be too much time for this when you are the attending and have sole 24 hour responsibility to the patient. Enjoy the time away from the hospital because there is still a buffer between you and the patient. Decide early on to have a life outside of the hospital and organize to do so in those limited number of hours. Be a competitive resident but save the leftover time for you.

> *I spent 6 years in residency and another 2 years in a research fellowship, equaling 8 years of postgraduate education, during which time I moved five times across the United States for a total of 18000 miles. Imagine the best years of my young life spent tired, in the hospital and living in moving boxes! Don't feel too sorry for me; despite the 1000 call nights I traveled to Asia three times during residency and even trekked around the Himalayan mountain range during my fourth postgraduate year. I put energy into establishing a supportive private life which served to balance the lack of support within the hospital environment. By placing equal importance on residency and my personal well-being, I have had many valuable experiences outside of medicine that have outlasted my medical training.*

Importance of first impressions

Generally, the early perceptions that the staff have of you in the first few months after 1 July set the tone on how you will be perceived throughout the residency. Guard those first impressions well. It is easier to maintain a positive impression than to change a negative one. Although it is possible to reverse a weak start, it takes more effort if you get off on the wrong foot. Later in practice, a strong first impression in the initial meeting will also impact on how the patient regards you. The way you come across may make a difference to whether or not that patient comes to accept you as their doctor. Pay attention to what constitutes *your* first impression including the nonverbal messages. Avoid inappropriate smiling and laughing during moments of nervousness or conflict. These mannerisms will weaken your stance in the professional arena. Work to combine a sharp appearance with a 'can do' attitude. Operate in the most positive form and get off to a great start.

Set up

Pick up the benefits package early or have it mailed to review what entitlements are included, for example eye care, medical and dental coverage, disability coverage and vacation time. Lots of residents miss these opportunities because they are not aware that they are entitled to them. Inquire about sick leave and maternity leave – key questions if you are planning a family. It is also a good idea to get the equal opportunity statement from the hospital. Find out *who* writes the schedule (usually the Chief Resident) and *when* requests for time off and vacation have to be submitted. Have payroll direct deposit the paycheck in your bank account.

Pay attention to the bulletin boards in the hospital, around the resident housing and college. When people move, especially around June, bargain furniture, electronics, books, etc. can be found. Find out what facilities and amenities are available at the hospital: child care, library, fax, medical arts department, computer services, copy machine, free meals and cafeteria hours. Assign yourself a locker and store the 'on call' bag in it. Books and tools tend to disappear in the hospital environment if not locked up. Keep these useful references available in the locker for quick referral during the middle of the night when other resources are closed.

Meet the hospital operators and ask for a directory of relevant phone numbers. Wear your name tag so they will remember you. Save time at night after bedding down by giving the operators the direct extension of the call room and having any pages come directly to the phone rather than to the beeper first. A wake-up call from an operator is the safest post call alarm clock. The operators often field calls from people requesting information on doctors. If they know you they might refer that call to your office and become a potential source of new patients for your future practice.

Personal safety

Generally hospitals are safe environments, but I have witnessed several instances that have made me understand that unfortunate things happen in there as they do on the street. Hospitals should provide for safety, but ensuring it often involves active inquiry on your part since no one is going around volunteering to take care of you. It is your right to insist on safe passage to and from the job with security rides or escorts. Be aware of your safety especially while roaming around the hospital at three in the morning.

> *During the fitful sleep of a typical night on duty in the hospital, I sensed a figure over my cot in the call room. In a second I was awake and realized it was a confused postoperative patient who was resistant to reason. I stood up on the cot and yelled. As I attempted to move toward the door, I fell onto him. This totally startled him and he became unable to grab or hit me because I was too close, literally on his chest. At this moment I leaped toward the door and got out. I ran down to the nurses station at the other end of the floor to find them unaware of any sound or disturbance. The next day the carpenters drilled a lock on the door.*
>
> *I am certain that had I not fallen on the intruder, I would have lost in a physical struggle with him. My close proximity to him negated his more powerful grabbing or striking ability and the element of surprise stunned this patient into immobility. So run away if you can but if you are blocked avoid a physical struggle and use your brain to outwit the attacker.*

Make sure there is a lock on the call room door. Place the phone within hands reach to pick up calls and to summon help. When walking in dark places, such as the parking garage or after closing at clinical offices, memorize the location of call phones and fire alarms. If threatened don't hesitate to pull one or trigger the alarm in a parked car by activating the motion detector. Break a window in a shop to activate the burglar alarm if necessary. Avoid the stairs late at night and instead use the elevators. Be careful about going into research areas during off hours as these are particularly under-patrolled by security; it's safer near the patients. If you have to go into an isolated area alone after hours stay behind a locked door with a phone. Tape the security phone number to the telephone. In an emergency, state your location first in case the call is cut off, at least someone will know where to find you. Something I couldn't afford as a resident but find mandatory as an attending is a cellular phone. Having the use of a cellular phone is an added safety factor. Call your service or friend to help if being followed, dial 911 directly or the hospital operators from the cellular phone. When called to the hospital in the middle of the night, alert someone that you are on the way and that if you fail to check in with them at a prefixed time they should become worried. Become familiar with the all-night stores along the route so that you might stop at one of these for help if being followed.

> *While doing a rotation in another city which happened to be on the opposite coast, I rented a room in the basement of a house with an entrance at the end of a lengthy bushy walkway. The medical service was very rigorous and I had to come and go at all hours of the night and early morning. I felt scared arriving home, dreading the long dark walk to an unlit apartment. A sympathetic friend lent me her stun gun after which I felt more confident and carried it every single day.*

Not once during my carreer did any of my colleagues or professors ever inquire about my safety as this is simply not an issue of concern for most men. For example, after an emergency operation at 2:30 am they would simply bark out orders on the patient and make the quickest exit. So do what you must to assure your safety and take care.

13

The white coat

If an object isn't secured to your person it is usually lost during a hectic night on call. The white coat becomes your portable medical office and each program should provide these free of charge. Since you will be living in these daily, make sure the coat fits well and looks neat. I still wear white coats because these protect my clothes, hold tools and the patients expect to see their doctor wearing one. Deciding what to carry in the pockets largely depends on what needs to be immediately available to complete the job. I carry a pocket-sized calendar book with me at all times in my coat and handbag. It serves to remind me of appointments, meetings, birthdays, important family dates and is a convenient way to track patients. It keeps me on schedule and is easy to refer to anytime in or out of the hospital. It's the one tool that I use the most to coordinate both professional and personal commitments. I also used this calendar book method to compile my list of patients for the Oral Boards requirements. Also carry in the coat's pockets: two pens, penlight, ruler, name tag, safety pin, pocket medical book and scissors. I used a small leather key pouch to carry hospital keys and meal money.

The anatomy of an 'on call' bag

The 'on call' bag holds those necessities that are required to keep you functioning normally while away from home and during residency for me this amounted to about 1000 nights. It is your bathroom, beauty salon and cafeteria in a bag. A properly packed bag can prepare you for a last minute date, feed you when all that is left in the coin machines is a pack of M & Ms and be a source of comfort on a long stressful call night. In planning the contents of the 'on call' bag consider what belongings you might include while packing for travel. Minimize the number of things moving between home and the hospital and carry into work only those items that need to be changed such as clothes or food.

14

Pick an inexpensive large zippered bag and store it in your locker. Hold clean supplies of spare underwear and support hose in it. Stock up on spare pens and other often-used medical supplies. Pack deodorant, cologne, soap, mouthwash and other female products, toothbrush and toothpaste. At a pinch some of these items can be found in the hospital utility room or gift shop. Hoard spare batteries in the 'on call' bag so precious sleep time won't be wasted hunting around the hospital at 3:00 am looking for a replacement battery for the beeper. A supply of snacks will come in handy if the cafeteria is closed and the only hope for eating is the vending machines. These should include dried foods such as soups and fruit, microwaveable meals, tea, pouches of hot chocolate and coffee. Service utensils and a microwave can be found at the nursing stations. Because I no longer take call in the hospital, my 'on call' bag has shrunk to the barest of essentials and is now kept in my desk at the office. For attending duties at hospitals in which I have neither an office nor locker, these necessities live in the trunk of the car.

In the dry air of the hospital it is important to maintain a practical beauty regimen suited to your needs. I recommend looking your best when you can and when it counts. The better you look, the better you'll be treated, not just in medicine but almost everywhere. Use up half spent cosmetics, hotel giveaways or sample make-up to fill a cosmetics pouch. Spend time fine tuning your make-up ritual to 10 minutes. If this is important to you get a beauty consultation and make-up lessons from the professionals. Make sure you have enough beauty supplies in the bag to prepare for an unexpected date. That way save time by going straight to the event without stopping at home first. Even now I keep a reserve of cosmetics in the office so I can go directly to any professional dinner or function. My personal make-up essentials: Elizabeth Arden pencil liner which has multiple uses, lipstick by Chanel and Great Lash Mascara by Maybelline.

Hair care should be kept to a simple style. Wash your hair on call nights only if the next day is the weekend and you are going

15

home, otherwise it wastes a lot of time and looks unprofessional walking into patients room with wet hair. Develop a relationship with a hair salon so that you can come for a styling when an important event arises at the last minute and they won't mind if you are occasionally delayed over a medical crises. Colored nail polish is acceptable in the hospital, but clear and non-opaque light colors last longer and the chips are harder to see. I wear a scent everyday and have never had a complaint (only positive responses). *Quality* cologne generally doesn't aggravate an allergy.

The professional uniform

It is more efficient to wear a uniform, which is probably why flight attendants and nurses do. I recommend wearing hospital uniforms on most days, it saves your own clothes, you don't have to do laundry and it simplifies life. With the hectic schedule of a neurosurgical resident I could sleep a few precious minutes longer and not waste a minute fumbling around in the closet deciding what to wear. At the very least get scrubs for overnight call. Scrubs are comfortable to sleep in, permissible to be seen in and the hospital does the washing.

When on call, dress in a style that doesn't interfere with your ability to get the job done in the quickest way. Shoes must be comfortable enough to be worn while running and climbing stairs. For six years I wore plastic clogs while on call. Wasting time with high heeled shoes, laces and buckles won't do in an emergency. Wearing support hose everyday at work is helpful. Ted stockings are also useful under scrubs to keep legs feeling energetic. Mail order support hose in bulk to save time and money.

Deny it or not, appearance counts. For those who have been buried in books for a decade or more, the fashion sense tends to atrophy. Personal style can enhance natural attractiveness or diminish it depending on the skill used to put yourself together. Men's suits are essentially a uniform. Find *your* professional uniform. In my life after residency I have fine-tuned my professional wardrobe and now expend very little effort on this. My closet is organized by season and I select what to wear with matching accessories for the entire week ahead, including all non-medical events. I wear mainly pants suits during the winter and skirt suits for the other seasons. I don't spend time co-ordinating different pieces together because the jacket is of identical material as the slacks or skirt. Clipping a beeper to the waist of a skirt or slacks is easier than finding a place on a dress to carry one.

Whatever you decide to wear, simplify the morning's decision as much as possible and save the major creativity for special occasions. Deviate from the uniform and dress for emphasis when it counts, such as on off-call days, for journal club or when giving grand rounds. Plan your outfit to incorporate after-work functions so that in case of an unplanned delay you can still preserve the evening plans by just changing an accessory such as a belt, earrings, adding heels, or switching from a beige shirt to a sparkly blouse for example. Store a pair of neutral hose in the office or the trunk of the car just in case. Learning to sequeway smoothly from work attire to evening wear eliminates squandering time on a trip home to change. If you don't have the time or the inclination to devise a well-coordinated wardrobe get ideas on professional dressing from Talbots Shops. All the pieces making up their outfits have been precoordinated and preaccessorized making the dresser's task easy. Personally I don't spend much money on clothing because I have learned a sense of what to wear and how to put it together. Some of my smartest and least expensive buys were found at resale shops.

Bag it

A well-made, elegant, black shoulder strap bag matches everything and since you will be using the bag daily invest in quality. I went through many bags before I finally found one that was large and strong enough to carry the required contents such as a phone, calendar book, journal, etc. and also contain the right number of compartments. My current shoulder bag is sturdy yet stylish enough to use for both work or evening activities. It is an integral piece of my uniform that is with me practically all year round.

Presentation attire

For presentations or talks wear professional dress suits that do not require any attention to look good. Avoid outfits that need adjustment or may fall in an embarrassing way. If the talk is in a large auditorium, bolder colors such as red or purple or simple geometrics will be attractive and might even make you more noticeable behind a podium or amid a sea of navy blue male suits. At a one-to-one interview, though, it's better to revert back to safe colors such as the all-time male favorite, navy blue. Wear heels that you can walk in and avoid any jewelry that will cause distracting noise or possibly fall off. Watch the nightly news and take a cue from the female newscasters and women politicians, notice how they put themselves together with accessories, scarves and colors. If it's a major extra-institutional talk, get your hair styled but don't look over-done. Pin the name tag on the *right* lapel, it's much easier for the other person to read and remember your name when shaking hands. While traveling to conferences or meetings dress professionally; you may end up sitting next to a colleague on the plane discussing job prospects.

The emergency dress

I own a few easy-to-wear professional dresses that I leave hanging in the closet for use on emergency calls at 2:00 am where I have to get to the hospital *now*. These dresses are always ready to be pulled off the hanger and thrown on. Dresses are easier than skirts, blouses or pants which have too many different pieces to coordinate. Keep the emergency dress in a place where it won't wrinkle and drape the matching hose over the hanger. Pick a dress that requires no accessories and is easily worn with black pumps. If the closet is arranged well it will be effortless to dress professionally in a hurry and you won't waste any time getting to the patient. I can be on my way to the hospital in 5 minutes with this method.

Diamonds and pearls

If there is a task that you must write daily such as progress notes, orders, history and physicals or sign outs, type or use a word processor to prepare a standard form on hospital stationary and photocopy several. Don't waste time on similar writing tasks day after day. The only additional required writing with these forms is that which is specific for the individual patient. Not only does it save time but it prevents forgetting important details.

The quickest way to review the medical chart of a patient is to read through the order sheets first and get a general picture of that patient's hospital course. These are generally written clearly and usually nothing happens to that patient unless it is ordered. Wrestling your way through unreadable progress notes may be reserved for eliciting further detailed information.

When doing call two nights in a row, write the next morning's progress notes just after midnight. If a change in a patient's status occurs, add an addendum. This frees up the day for other duties.

When a patient asks questions regarding her condition resist the urge to offer your interpretation of the illness. Instead always begin the answer by inquiring what the attending doctor has already told her. Have the patient explain in her own words what she knows. Then repeat what she has said, using some of the same phrases, to build upon in providing an explanation. This will reinforce what the attending physician has previously discussed with the patient and minimize confusion. Never appear to contradict the attending in the eyes of his/her patient. A patient who receives differing accounts of their condition from well-meaning but inexperienced medical staff can become very anxious and angry. I have spent much time backtracking and doing damage control for residents and fellow physicians who took the liberty of rendering an explanation of my patients' status without first asking what their understanding of the situation was. Watch how experienced staff talk to their patients and note how a difficult predicament is diffused.

Never discuss therapeutic strategy at the patient's bedside. Move out of the patient's room to openly review and debate the options. It is important to maintain a cohesive 'team' appearance in front of the patient. The patient may lose confidence in their care if he senses that there is confusion or conflict regarding the treatment.

Useful tips

- ❑ Alcohol fades ink stains from pens

- ❑ Hydrogen peroxide removes blood

- ❑ Tongue depressors can be used as spoons or stirrers

- ❑ Spinal needles with syringes can be used to transfer precious liquids such as perfume from one bottle to another without spilling a drop, or to deposit liquid in a hard to reach place

- ❑ Hospital ID bands can be used to label a stethoscope and as luggage tags

- ❑ Duoderm makes great blister protection

- ❑ Surgical scrub brush can be used to comb the hair

- ❑ Forceps and nylon suture can repair a hem

- ❑ Examination table paper or bubble wrap make interesting giftwrap at a pinch

- ❑ Boxes for mailing or packing can be found by the hundred in central supply

- ❑ In an emergency surgilube makes passable hair gel

❑   To have a readily available ruler, pre-measure a common hospital item like a gauze sponge. That way you will at least have a reference, which can be substituted for a ruler, especially in a sterile field

On call open time

During my 1000 nights on call in the hospital there were long periods when all the patients were taken care of and there was simply open time. Always prepare for such periods as this is a hidden resource that most residents waste and although you may be in the hospital this is time that is yours. Consult your 'to do' list and start to knock off a few items. Use your open time while trapped in the hospital to make phone calls, mail order gifts (flowers for Mother's Day, etc.) and clothes, write letters, write presentations, address Christmas cards, schedule appointments, order theater tickets, research or write articles, work out in the physical therapy department, speak with the nurses; it's amazing what it is possible to accomplish if organized ahead of time. Photocopy chapters from the text books and bring these sheets along to work. After reading these simply throw them away instead of carrying the heavy books back and forth. Even now I carry photocopies of current articles to read while standing in grocery lines, bank lines, while being put on hold, on the plane or while waiting anywhere. Keep-up with current events by watching television in the lounges and reading the newspapers or magazines that patients discard. Some of my best recipes, child care lessons and household organizational methods come from magazines that patients have given to me. Don't close yourself out to investigating other areas of life even while on the job. Incorporate the effective use of open time into your life to be applied where ever you may be. This thinking was the driving force behind the writing of this book, the bulk of which was written in airports and on plane rides.

3   Life support

The women around us

Just because there are other women working with you doesn't mean that the job is any easier or that you have company. It depends on how the women are and how they interact together. Even though there are many women around the hospital in different roles, women physicians often feel isolated. For any number of reasons often we don't get the support from other women that would seem logical in the best interest of the gender. So there we work surrounded by other women, alone.

If you interact with the other women the way that the men do, you will be far less successful than they. Treat the women, no matter what level they are, as you have treated all women throughout life. Women do not respond to female authority in the same manner that they do to male.

The pink collar patrol: secretaries

I have had some fun and supportive relationships with secretaries over the years. Secretaries can be an extremely good source of political information and generally are privy to inner sanctum data. If they like you, some of this useful information may be passed to you. Because women generally relate to one another by trading personal information, it's best to keep the relationships superficial or formal and not engage in personal discussion, since anything revealed could circulate around the office to the chief. Treat the secretaries well and avoid conflict. Be careful not to antagonize the secretaries; they might obstruct and sabotage your future especially at the residency level. They can have enormous influence on their bosses who are also your superiors. A professor's loyalty will usually remain on the side of the secretary should you find yourself pitted against one of them.

These women must think of you positively because they are vital to the handling of logistical procedures during residency and the certification process that follows. The letters of recommendation that are required for hospital privileges, jobs and board certification will be typed by these secretaries. Remember, that you are only in residency for a brief period of time and in a sense passing through; the secretaries on the other hand are there to stay. For this transitory interval they have power over you and they know it. If you are mystified at the clout they wield over a mere resident, take heart, the relationships become less puzzling as you ascend the medical ladder. The most cooperative relationships I've had with women in these supporting roles are those in which I am the direct provider of their paychecks. You hold power over them and they know it. As their boss the circumstances shift and because of their proximity to you they may have access to private information, so continue to maintain a formal relationship and dutifully remember Secretaries Day (April) and other important dates. Gift ideas include: certificates for manicures or facials, designer candy, desk radios, potted plants, expensive picture frames, crystal vase with flowers, fancy pen, money, time off, computer lessons.

The nurses

Nurses are an excellent source of female interest information. They generally live in the area and can lend advice for improving one's life away from the hospital. The nurses can suggest a good dentist, cleaners, beauty salon, house cleaner, child care solutions, where to eat, restaurants that deliver, where to shop, etc. Tap them for these types of facts.

The nurses have the potential to really help women, but if they do not like you personally they could possibly hinder your career at that hospital. Never underestimate their ability to make life miserable during residency and especially encroach upon the number of sleep hours. In an argument with a nurse or other health professional focus only on what is in the best interest of the *patient*. Limit the discussion to medical issues and use the following phrase often 'In the best interest of the patient...'. You must keep the dialog centered specifically around the patient and avoid any deterioration into the personal zone.

Just accept the fact that the way the nurses interact with you may differ from a man in a similar position. You will work harder than the men in the first several months, after which nurses soften and may begin to help you. Discover the approach that works to get the most assistance from the nurses. Start by learning and addressing them by their names. Treating the nurses with respect by demonstrating that you value their input and opinions generally saves the day and eventually they will come around. Nurses regard doctors who treat patients well as allies and a reputation of this kind will help win them over. Ironically, if the nurses feel comfortable, you may even be asked to do extra work because they imagine you're more 'approachable' than the men or 'she won't say no'. If it happens a few times, go along with it as a favor to them but if the requests become habitual, take action. The way to handle this is to politely but consistently redirect their efforts back to the responsible party. Avoid letting anyone take advantage of your goodwill by loading you down with another's duties just because you're 'nice'.

Show your appreciation to these women by remembering them on special occasions – something I was better at than my male cohorts. Nurses burn out on food over the holidays so if you're giving candy do it early in the season and don't forget to deliver something for every shift. Other ideas: barrel of popcorn, coffee maker, packages of microwavable popcorn, tea, hot chocolate, designer coffee, radio, mugs, an in-service on a topic of their choosing, flowers.

Ms M.D.

I hope you know other women physicians who are mutually supportive of one another. Some of these friendships have been the dearest throughout my career because we understand each other's lives better than anyone else. On the other side, I have been in situations with women where there just wasn't any common ground. If you find yourself in a similar environment, forget the notion that in order to work with these women you must also be friends. Avoid revealing too much personal data with those who you know very superficially and cannot trust. If you need to decompress and there is no one to trust, get an outside opinion.

> *I knew a woman surgeon who commiserated openly about being alone with no mate and few friends, all she had was her job; which she was very respected for. We became friends and I saw her on numerous social occasions. During one of these occasions while helping another nonmedical friend to decorate her home, the surgeon started to take charge and to order people about, as though 'she was still in the operating room'. To my second friend who didn't care a wit about her surgical ability, she was only a woman with obnoxious behavior. After several repeat performances I realized that the woman doctor was unable to distinguish the lady from the surgeon. She wasn't a mean or unkind friend, it's just that her view of the world and her place in it had become warped.*

Women are supremely helpful in areas outside the male domain like pregnancy, child care, harassment, appearance tips, discrimination, etc. Having another woman in the program or a woman attending doesn't guarantee a confidante or role model, however. Often the women are so muddled with their own concerns that they can't help much. Some women have been through an exhausting lonely struggle only to end up holding precarious appointments, so don't expect *more* from a senior woman than you would from a man. Even if a woman doesn't actually do anything specifically to benefit you, just the fact that she is there and visible helps.

Learn by observation: how she carries herself, how she interacts with others, how she handles conflicts and how successful she is in her career. Remember that the choices she has made in her life may not agree with the plans for yours. There exists a generational divide that separates the pioneers from the followers. Many of the younger women are not willing to accept the sacrifices that the senior women have had to make and this should not be held against anyone. I've learned as much from the mistakes of other women as I have by their successes. Although there is no one single person I would emulate there is a part of many that I admire. I am a composite of many, many women and men whom I've known over the years, and some have been outside medicine. Incorporate those qualities that fit and make them a role model for yourself. Remember it's not that we need more female role models, we need women at every level supporting us.

Some of the most mystifying women I have known are those whose status is in some way related to the men they associate with. For example those women whose fathers, husbands or lovers are doctors in powerful positions. Although many of these women are highly qualified, they have often scaled the medical power structure much more smoothly than the rest of us and I am disappointed to have observed that a few of them have been the least helpful of all. It is logical to think that they would want to use their privileged and somewhat protected standing to assist others, but I am baffled to discover that these women often hold other women to a different standard and are harder on their female colleagues than the men. I support women moving ahead, even with this type of advantage, but I wish that these women would not think of their position as a limited resource and have the confidence to share instead of hoard.

The men around us

Women have never been 'one of the boys'. Male residents do not juggle as many roles as women and may be clueless regarding the pressures we face in our private lives. When these matters, for example pregnancy, begin to influence a male resident's work-load, at the best he may remain neutral or he may resent and undermine you. Even if men did understand the issues that women have to deal with, most of them are not capable of bolstering us up with comforting heart-to-heart talk. Instead, men express their support by action and doing. You know that the fellow resident approves of you when he offers to pitch in on a busy day at the hospital by volunteering to do an extra history and physical, run a blood sample to the lab or scrub with the Chief. Show your mutual support for him by returning the favor when he needs one.

Learn the ways of male interaction by watching how they talk to each other and imitate this when speaking with men. Try to minimize detailed explanations and instead get to the point first and fast, then come back and elaborate if necessary. Avoid qualifiers like 'This may sound dumb' or 'I may be wrong'. A man hears this as 'I am dumb so don't listen to what I'm saying' or 'I am wrong so what I'm saying can't be right'. State your opinion firmly and positively. Start bragging about yourself as the 'boys' do.

While doing a rotation in a program on the opposite coast, during Morbidity and Mortality Rounds, the Chief asked me to explain my actions on a case that I had handled. I steeled myself, ready to engage alone in a losing verbal discussion with the Head Man when before I could respond, two male voices piped up and answered before me in support of my clinical judgment. Imagine my surprise when the discussion was suddenly steered away from me by the simple interjections of two colleagues who otherwise respected my work, something that never happened at my 'parent institute'. Why the different response? It had to do with how the Chiefs at each hospital regarded women. My first Chief barely tolerated having women in his program but the Chief at the hospital where I was a visiting resident sent out a message loud and clear that we had every right to be there. When they start to defend you, they really like you and it is a great place to be.

Listen to the residents discussing each attending and decide who among these could be a possible supporter since you will need several. Because you looked up the faculty in the *Index Medicus* before the interview, you will have some knowledge of their interests and recent publications. Academics like to be asked genuine questions about their work so use this as an entrée to dialog. Do not get left out of the after-hours mentoring loop where the informal networking takes place just because you are a woman. Lots of valuable information is traded at the squash game or beer after rounds. Eating lunch alone won't advance your standing so make it a point to eat with other members of the medical team. Even if they don't talk to you directly, just by listening you can still garner valuable information. If an attending makes a genuine effort to invite you for lunch, coffee, etc, *go* because after relaxing they tend to 'spill' the ins and outs of program politics. Getting to know attendings this way makes them more likely to give you a break in the future, like letting you operate, backing you during Morbidity and Mortality conference, including you as an author in a paper, or assisting in the job search.

Take an interest in knowing those who you can relate to. If anyone is doing work in areas that sincerely interest you, get involved with them. Finding common ground with an attending can lead to a helpful relationship which can continue to provide career advice even after residency. Concentrate the efforts on those who like you and don't waste precious time trying to change the others. No matter how dismal the situation will seem, or how isolated you feel, there will be at least one attending who will be of help. Although many women have great intentions regarding the mentoring of others, they may not be in a powerful enough position to make a political difference in another's career. The shrewdest alliance to have is with a strong male mentor who believes in you and has a vested interest in seeing you succeed. For a long and substantial relationship with a male mentor, you need to get along with his wife. If his wife is insecure, his ability to help may be thwarted. Guard against this by having several mentors at once.

4 Glass scalpel

Our comrades in business call it the 'glass ceiling', that invisible barrier which prevents women from reaching the higher echelons. In medicine, women have to struggle with the 'glass scalpel'. On the surface the scalpel appears to look like any other but no matter how skillful we are at cutting and how great the results are, the scalpel eventually shatters. In the long run, it just doesn't cut the same for us as it does for the men. It is not only those in positions of authority but also those below us who in not supporting our ascent, prevent us from moving forward. The truth is that in most of the areas of academic medicine the dominant culture is still male and although personally we interact well with men, in the professional setting the rules and language are all theirs. This is not likely to change for a while. In order to succeed, it may be necessary for you to gain an understanding of the dynamics within the male culture. To determine whether or not there are any glass scalpels lurking in your program, consider the following.

The policies of a program, written and unwritten, are set by the person at the top. The viewpoint of the Chief regarding women will be emulated, to a large extent, by those men beneath him. If the Chief has an old-fashioned view, his subordinates may have little respect for the skill or feelings of women and you might be alone in trying to solve any problems in this male–female minefield. Men more easily grasp the reality of these situations from a woman's perspective if it has affected them personally first. If the chief or supervisor has heard a similar story at home from a woman close to him (wife, lover, sister, daughter), there is a chance that this man may understand your plight. An enlightened Chief, who will not tolerate harassment or discrimination in his program, places you in a very fortunate situation. When such a man values your work consider yourself in a shielded position.

Harassment

There is currently a heightened sensitivity about sexual harassment in the hospital environment. Because it has affected many working women there is other more sophisticated literature available for guidance. Familiarize yourself with this material and read the equal opportunity statement from the institute. There is no *one* way to handle this unwanted attention which may require an individual judgment call. Here is my own brief advice on this issue. If you are the target of unsolicited sexual advances, threats, gestures, etc. set the person straight immediately, then document the events by keeping a log and have witnesses present if possible. Strengthen the complaint with physical evidence: cellular phone records, operator assisted pages, calls to the service or answering machine and e-mail can be used to support the case. Keep anything that is written to you. Seek professional advice from the Equal Opportunity Office early and bring in the supportive material. Depending on the philosophy of the department, and who the harasser is, discussing this with the Chief may or may not help. Gauge this by yourself. Men respond to facts, so if you support the complaint clearly and unemotionally with evidence, the Chief may become sufficiently convinced to intervene.

Call the local branch of the American Medical Women's Association (AMWA) and the American Association of Medical Colleges to find out how other women have dealt with this and what the options are. Use humor, a rational 'get the data' approach, letting the boys or superior males fix it, do nothing or leave; whatever is necessary to minimize any further loss. If that fails to correct the situation and your career is at stake get advice from the outside and hire a lawyer to stop it. This does not necessarily imply a lawsuit but an alerting letter on your behalf from an attorney can put the party on notice and have the matter preempted. This may stop the harassment but make life in that residency uncomfortable. Still, do what you have to do to finish training. A lawsuit is the last resort and should be reserved for dire situations as it is time consuming and expensive. Even with a legal victory you will have lost much. If you have a short period of time left in the residency then your best option may be to avoid the harasser until you leave.

Discrimination

Gender discrimination is the seemingly small inequities like making you invisible and leaving you out, tactless jokes, offensive behavior, intimidating posture and hostile attitudes that over time amount to a mountain. This is more difficult to deal with because it's harder to prove and usually gets bounced back to the side of the complainer who is labeled as *overly sensitive*. Most men won't understand this type of situation and will tend to dismiss or minimize the complaints. It is possible to have no male allies on this issue, but the commonality with women throughout the workplace will make up for it. Many women have had experience of this type of treatment and it has left them bitter. Do not become convinced that what is happening is your fault because it occurs to many minorities in all walks of life and discrimination is a symptom of the immaturity of that particular organization. If the situation is unbearable, document it, see a lawyer or counselor and ask other women for support and advice. Fellow women physicians have been morally supportive to me regarding this matter since it has invariably happened to them. Become mindful of it from the start and safeguard against it by allying with those who are on your side.

In surgical training, this bias is a particularly dangerous issue when, as a resident, you are reliant on someone (usually a man) to turn the case over so that your skills can mature. If you are not doing the same thing that a male is permitted to do, call the attending on it and state firmly that you would like to do more in the next case together. Ask for constructive advice on how to accomplish this in the upcoming operation. Appeal to the attending's sense of fairness since

33

most men will understand this logic. It is easy to say nothing but your skills will suffer for it. If it is repeated a second time and nothing further can be gained by just watching, scrub with someone else and don't let the situation ruin the training. Find the person who will teach you to become the best doctor possible.

Keep in mind that subordinate males can make your life more miserable than those in authority. Less senior male staff will constantly test you, challenging you even in those areas that they know very little about. A junior male who is insubordinate has taken the message from those in authority positions that it is okay to act in such a manner. This is an extremely difficult position to be in as you will be undermined every step of the way by him. Again, if not supported by the chief, your authority will be continually questioned by those below, no matter how good a doctor you are.

Salty tears

If you are ever reduced to tears, immediately excuse yourself to regain composure and pick up the discussion at a later time. Men are very uncomfortable with tears and become annoyed at crying in the job setting. Your male colleagues will not respond favorably to tears, as I have learned the hard way. If the residency has worn you out and friends have heard the story too many times, get private professional counseling. Think of it as an investment in your mental health and career longevity. Do not put it on the residency record since any documented psychological treatment may disqualify you for disability insurance.

Making rain

Moving up the career ladder doesn't make you immune to the multitude of inequities that happen to women as we venture forward. I've known some women who have breezed through residency unscathed only to find that as practitioners they were not getting the same number of referrals that a male at the same level received. The world hasn't changed, but I have. I now have the confidence to understand that when I am slighted it's not a personal reflection and that that person has the problem, not me. I pick my battles and let others pass. I learned from many mistakes how to move around obstacles in a manner that is acceptable. Value the importance of having allies who can understand your vision and who will help to pass those small minds standing in the foreground blowing steam. Avoid those who wish you ill, you don't need them and they will not help you. Use your woman's intuition to find solutions to the bias that arises while keeping focused on what needs to be done not on what they are doing. The options are greater as an attending so do not tolerate an untenable situation. Don't be afraid to leave if those in the workplace are reminders of life in residency or worse.

> *In practice, I resolved repeated disrespect from a senior attending (whose best friend was the Chief of the service) by alerting the president of the hospital, one of my very strong supporters. How did I get the president on my side? I became a rainmaker for the hospital. I bring in dollars and they know it. Bottom line advantage wipes away gender politics in a flash.*

Preparing for an encounter with the glass scalpel

In medicine, as in many professional sectors, the dominant culture is male and we are simply visitors. In this male world women are too quiet and too over-prepared. The professional world expects women to be so, and as we see it, is also less forgiving of our mistakes. Men are not spending nearly as much time in preparation and often just 'wing it' and do okay. Besides, men are forgiven their mistakes. Women are terrified of failing and looking 'stupid' so we spend excessive time preparing. A disorganized and unprepared woman will have a difficult time succeeding but not so for the men.

35

Speak up and shatter the glass scalpel

Communication is very important in medicine, both with our peers and with patients. In order to move in the male domain you must understand how men speak with one another and become fluent in male-talk. If you need to discuss a complicated situation with a man, use terms or analogies that incorporate military or sports expressions. They will visualize the concept faster. For example:

The actual predicament

A female attending at a trauma hospital is supervisor to three male house officers. The Chief of the service spends 95% of his time at another hospital, the parent institute, and has very little idea of how the service actually functions. Insubordinate behavior occurs frequently and when the woman physician reports this to her Chief he pays her lip service but actually does nothing. In fact, at times he even plays to the side of the junior male medical staff behind her back. This goes on for one year and as a result the house officers get the message that their negative behavior toward the female supervisor is not going to be disciplined. The lack of support from the Chief undermines the effectiveness of the woman and sends the message to the subordinates that it is okay not to follow her orders.

How to communicate about this with a male

When the general (Dr Chief) is stationed in Washington, DC, and the lieutenant (female physician supervisor) is with the troops in the trenches of Georgia (a) the troops will get away with what they can because the highest authority is seldom present and (b) when the troops get the message that the general doesn't support the lieutenant, the troops will mutiny.

Cut through the circuitous details and give a man the story in the way he understands.

One of the most valuable skills you can develop is effective verbal expression and confident public speaking. If your position includes frequent speaking, get a professional evaluation and training from a speech coach. Nothing impresses an audience more than a speaker with a cohesive and well-organized delivery. Sell yourself with verbal talent and the ability to competently handle questions. Begin practicing early in your career by reciting histories and physicals during medical school to an audience.

Start speaking now: the last-minute presentation

You are ordered to give a 15–20 minute topical presentation and have one post call night to prepare. Look up the subject in the most recent textbook. Use the format in the text as the guide to organizing the talk and write this out as an outline on the chalk board before beginning or prepare overhead transparencies. While referring to the outline, give the facts, filter the talk with references listed at the end of the chapter and repeat the facts again.

With more advanced warning, look up the references listed in the text, review the abstracts and incorporate these at the appropriate time. Refer to a case which typifies the subject matter spoken about and reemphasize the key points of this medical entity. Make copies of applicable articles and give these as handouts after the presentation. It's a good idea to start accruing papers that are relevant during residency. Keep these filed under suitable topics and titles for easy referral. Hand these out to other staff members as the subject arises. Stamp your name on it so whoever reads it will know where it came from.

Grand rounds

Not many of us are such dynamic speakers that we can give a presentation which maintains audience interest without the assistance of visual aids. When giving grand rounds prepare something visual to augment the presentation. Get the medical arts department involved to create slides or do your own with Powerpoint® (Microsoft®). If slides are impossible, prepare overhead projector transparencies. Rehearse the order of your talk and make sure to have it well-coordinated with the slides. Don't use two slide projectors unless you are extremely well-prepared or are very experienced. Use the slides or transparencies as notes and expand the major ideas listed on these with further detailed talk. With the slides properly prepared there should be no reason to look at a piece of paper. One slide should correspond to about 1–2 minutes of talk. A common mistake people make is to put too much on one slide. The audience gets lost between reading the slide and listening to the speaker. Watch how others give presentations and copy the styles that are most effective, including mannerisms. Never go beyond the allotted time, the audience resents it.

Keep the slides simple and embellish main words with talk. Use labels, key phrases and lists of bulleted words. For example: 'Symptoms: headache, nausea, vomiting'. Large lettering that is bright yellow, bright green or black works from all distances. Never use red lettering or blue lettering on a black background, it's difficult to read from the back of the room. A light blue background is pleasing since it is a favorite color of many. Keep the slides uniformly colored but simple. Avoid overdoing the backgrounds with too much geometry and vertiginous design. If a key word is used throughout the talk keep it consistently the same color in all the slides. Mark every slide to indicate the correct placement in a projector carousel.

If one of the attending has a particularly interesting present-ation ask to copy their slides. It is less expensive to copy slides than to create new ones. Start to accrue a collection of slides while in residency. These can be useful in providing the background for presentations to promote your practice later. Develop talks that can be delivered on a moment's notice to different audiences that may be pertinent to building presence in your specialty. It is much simpler to give the same talk many times to a different audience than to give different talks to the same audience.

National conference talks

A presentation at a national meeting can get you noticed, especially if looking for employment after residency. Prepare well and try to maintain a relaxed appearance that will exude confidence. This is convincing to anyone evaluating you for a possible job. Some of my actor friends swear by propranolol to get through opening night butterflies. Rehearse the talk in a trial run at your own institute and ask for feedback. Prior to the talk, become familiar with the podium when the room is empty. Check to see if there are stairs, examine the slide projector controls, the pointer and the microphone. If the microphone clips to your lapel, then place it on the side which will be closest to the slide screen while you are speaking. If the slide screen is on the left, clip the microphone on the left lapel adding another good reason to wear a suit. If the microphone is attached to the podium, position it so that it rests at the chin level and not directly in front of the mouth thereby avoiding annoying noise from exhaled air when speaking. Do not waste time fumbling with these devices as you initiate the presentation. Arrange to have the title slide showing on the screen while approaching the podium. It allows the audience to see the title of the talk and to focus on the presenter.

In a 15 minute or shorter talk it is critical to avoid distractions and interruptions or the main idea of the presentation will be lost. A short talk needs to flow smoothly and clearly to be effective. Don't attempt to discuss too much information in a short time-frame. Limit the main points to three – that way the audience will have learned at least that much. Too much information will overwhelm the audience and instead of learning three important points from the talk they may be turned off or confused by the facts. The presentation has better choreography if the slides are controlled by the speaker so that the tempo of the talk isn't disrupted by signaling for a slide change.

Packing for a conference: take carry-on luggage and hold the presentation material (slides, video) with you. Plan your conference attire around a color theme in order to avoid taking too many pairs of shoes or different accessories. Call the hotel ahead of time and inquire about work-out facilities and beauty amenities.

International conference talks

The international conferences tend to run less smoothly as compared with those at home, especially in the Third World. Be prepared and don't rely too much on slides, microphones or any sophisticated electronics. Be aware that projectors or other devices may be radically different from those in the USA. Bring along as many presentation aides as possible including a pointer, some information on both slides and transparencies, etc. While attending a meeting in China I decided at the last minute to completely alter my prepared talk in order to better fit the audience's interest. This was easily done because I had packed extra slides on the topic.

The question period

The question period can be as unsettling as the talk itself, and being able to field questions at the end of a presentation is another skill. Firmly state that all questions are to be held until the end to avoid interrupting the integrity of the talk. Try to anticipate the questions ahead of time and prepare answers for these. Pay attention to the character of the questions. By evaluating what is asked, gauge how effective you were in getting the points across and therefore what may or may not need to be revised in the talk. If you have given the same presentation several times and a similar question keeps arising consider incorporating the answer in the body of your talk because this may signify an area of confusion. If a question is asked that seems puzzling or off the mark, ask for it to be repeated or rephrase it in a manner that you know the answer to. When an audience member asks a series of questions, concentrate on answering the first or easiest one. If they follow up, ask for a repeat or just move on to another questioner as smoothly as possible. If the question is too difficult, or the asker is hostile, say 'That's a good question' (give a compliment) then say 'We don't have enough time to go into the details but I'd be glad to speak with you about it afterward'. Don't let anyone intimidate you with a question, retain control of the presentation by deciding what will be answered based on your strengths and knowledge of the subject. Maintain composure and certainty through to the end.

Research opportunities

If you are determined to strengthen your CV, investigate research options during residency and discover what undertaking such work entails. In some ideal residencies a research year is built in or optional. Unless there is dedicated time off, it's not easy to complete a basic science study during residency but a clinical investigation can be completed. Examine the work already in progress at the institute and decide if you are interested in participating. Becoming part of an already existing project will yield greater results than if you have to start from just an idea. If given the option to leave your institute to do research elsewhere, *go*. Things are often done differently at outside institutes and you will become all the more experienced for having observed another medical approach to the same problem. The wider the exposure, the more versatile a physician you will be.

An attending may approach you to co-author an article with him/her. This is a great opportunity to learn the ropes of writing articles for biomedical journals under the guidance of someone who has experience. After the first few articles writing becomes simpler and you can continue the process on your own. Clarify exactly what needs to be done, which journal the article is intended for, what order the authors' names will be in, then put it in writing in a thank-you note. Keep a copy of this in your files to avoid confusion later. Publications will invigorate a CV and enhance a career no matter what path is followed, but if an academic career is in the future, publishing on demand is a given. Aggressively submit abstracts for conferences in order to obtain priority for attending these. Conferences are principal places to network, to job hunt and to get your name out there. Besides, it's time away from the grueling hospital and the residency program should pay for the trip.

5 Procedures

> *When a male junior attending walked into the operating room on a case that I was completing during my chief residency and said to the whole room 'You hold the instruments like a woman' I wondered if my style was different from the other residents. Now that I have proven my operating skills here's what I have observed about myself: the woman surgeon who operates like a woman.*

Do not apologize too early

Working as a teacher with male and female residents I've observed that women tend to be more hesitant about doing a procedure for the first time. Women nonverbally or otherwise broadcast the fact that 'I've never done this before' much louder than men. With men you might never know that this is the first time for them, as they simply jump in without ever mentioning it and most of the time all goes well. When a woman states up-front that she has never done such a procedure before, the male attending reads this insecurity as inability and is therefore also hesitant to let her do anything. As a consequence she might never do it, thus ending up left behind. Follow the lead of the men and don't apologize too soon. If someone has decided to let you do a procedure and you have confidence in their guidance, go with it – chances are it will be successful. Then write it down in a journal listing the steps needed to complete a specific procedure or operation in 'cookbook' format. Refer to this prior to doing it next time.

Overcoming the strength factor with finesse

The difference between men and women becomes noticeable the more that the field involves physical strength. Surgery is one of the few professional physical events where males and females intermingle at the same level. Many women don't have the same upper body strength as their male counterparts. To accomplish a similar task women must rely on technique and leverage to overcome force, especially when upper body strength is necessary. This factors into surgical training since we rely mostly on males to teach us. When men teach men the instructions are clear and direct because of similar strengths and anatomy. Although there are many fine male educators, they may be unaware of the best way to teach women the same procedure within the ergonomics of the female body. The men are operating using their normal physical strength which often exceeds that of the female resident they are teaching.

> *The best surgical assistants I have ever operated with have been other women because we innately understood each other's abilities. I knew how to assist her when she was struggling to do a particular maneuver as she knew for me also. It all has to do with the shared physical strengths.*

Before starting any procedure including arterial blood gas sticks, intravenous catheter placement, blood drawing, central line access, foley insertion, or other, set the lighting, arrange the instruments and then get into a comfortable, advantageous position. Put the table or bed at the appropriate height *for you* ahead of time. This preparation ritual will give you the utmost chance of success and cause less trauma to the patient. Always approach the procedure from the angle that affords the most control, namely if you are right-handed, attempt the procedure from the side, usually the patient's right, that gives your dominant hand the best advantage. When being taught a procedure or operation it is critical to engage in the maneuver from your most favorable position and not necessarily that of the instructor's. What feels perfectly normal to a 6 foot tall man probably will be an awkward and unsafe position for you to do that procedure on

44

the patient. If the male instructor is taller, either lower the table to a level that you are comfortable with or stand on step stools. Clogs can also painlessly add 2 inches to height.

In cases that require upper body force, I exploit leverage to my benefit. I keep the table lower than most male surgeons, thereby allowing the use of my entire body during the execution of an operation instead of just the hands and forearms that the men can get away with. I tend to move and change my body position often to give the arms and hands the best physical advantage. Men move less and are able to do more from a single stance because of their increased upper body strength.

> *As I began using power tools for bone removal in my spinal surgical cases the strength requirement vanished although I still feel that a lower table yields more control and that a soft touch leads to better results than a power move.*

Ironically those fields that require fine detail work may give women with smaller hands the ergonomic advantage over men.

Tools and space

Most of the surgical instruments that we use were designed for men by men. Since women are newcomers to the field of surgery, we haven't yet begun to modify the implements as professional women have done with tennis rackets, golf clubs, etc. In these professional sports the critical tools are gender different. My chief wore a size 8 glove and I a size 6. The tools that fit his hands perfectly felt like heavy unbalanced spears in mine. Therefore when a male attending gives a female resident an instrument to commence surgery on the patient she is disadvantaged at the onset. To begin with the table is set to his liking and may be too high for her. She may not be comfortable with the tool and may look clumsy or slow which leads the attending to wonder if she's capable or coordinated enough to do the procedure. The tools may simply be too big for her hands to control adequately. If an attending puts a tool in your hand and it feels awkward, move your hand along the handle to achieve a better leverage point. You need not hold the tool in the same place that he did since your hand size is different. Try a variety of tools and seek those that work best for you. You may discover that you need a totally different set of instruments to do the same procedure. Given the correct tools, your technique will match up but it's your responsibility to find these and to experiment with what works. Don't be afraid to reinterpret rules and invent your way of doing things if the result is going to be better for the patient.

Men tend to dominate the most critical position in the surgical field even without knowing it, so they often need to be reminded that it is mandatory for you to operate standing directly in front of the patient in the place where the move can be executed safely.

> *I remember an overweight attending who because of his size monopolized the entire space at the patient's head. He placed a power tool in my hand and told me to open the cranium. When I asked him to move over so I could come closer to the patient, he said 'I won't let you do anything wrong', but he refused to budge. I declined using the tool in a position which would compromise my ability to do the procedure.*

Men are not used to letting a women occupy the center of the field even when they are only assisting in the surgery. As an attending I have literally had to push them out of the way. Position your body optimally, find the tools that allow the best performance for the patient and operate the way that feels the most relaxed even if it means changing the way you've been taught.

6 Your recovery room

Home is your sanctuary to relax in and to just be a normal woman. You may not be able to control all that happens at the workplace but you *are* in command at home, so when the door is closed lock those residency hassles out. This is where friends and supporters gather to boost you, no one comes unless invited. You are boss here, so organize the home so that those precious hours are well spent. Having a great home that is all you, whether it's a house, apartment or even a room, allows recovery from the rigors of medicine and therefore permits a higher level of functioning in that residency.

> *After years of using cardboard boxes for tables and stands I decided that because I was going to be in one place for more than a year I would bite the bullet and finally buy real furniture. My apartment became a place that I loved to be in. I filled it with my favorite colors and precious reminders of life away from medicine. My apartment was such a joy that it helped to neutralize the negative aspects of residency. Although I doubt if anyone else felt this way, to me it was a wonderful apartment that would literally transport me far away from residency. I learned that I value the aesthetics of my personal surroundings much more than I realized in my younger days.*

Work toward feeling good about this part of life and look forward to coming home, do it because it will be important to a balanced survival.

To perform your job well, take good care of yourself first and keep those things that mean the most to you personally high on the priority list. Hoard time away from the hospital for doing

47

what makes you happiest. Discover ways to relieve stress that work. Optimize your surroundings to complement your lifestyle, the hectic schedule and the needs of your family. In order to do this, organize to make home efficient but pleasant, but be aware that the importance placed on the following issues will vary individually. Here are some ideas for making those precious hours at home stretch the furthest.

Organizing home: low tech

Jump-start the morning by having the closet well-organized with clothes laid out for the entire week ahead, a make-up routine that is honed to the essentials and a breakfast that takes minutes to prepare. Arrange the alarm clock away from the bed so that you must physically leave the bed to turn it off, otherwise it's too tempting to fall back asleep on those post-call mornings. Set out any items that you have to take to work the next morning the night before. On workday mornings there is no time for creativity so try to develop a morning routine. Let these tasks become routine and minimize the stress of a busy morning by maintaining a structured and well-organized setting.

Use high tech to make life easier

The phone is the vital link to the hospital, so plan to have every extra function available on the line. My phone numbers have always been unlisted so that any possible undesirable callers will have a harder time finding me. Call waiting is essential, especially if call is taken from home. Conference capability is useful when a decision involves the input of several people. As an ambitious attending/business-woman, I now have two phone lines at home, one for business and the other for calls. Using a smart box I can route faxes, the computer modem and teleradiology via the business line. Install an answering machine that can be remotely accessed to monitor messages from the hospital when on call or even while traveling. The beeper lives in my purse near the bed in case the phone fails. I was once so tired after a call in the middle of the night that I put the phone down wrong and anyone calling got a busy signal. Luckily the beeper next to the bed rang with the next call.

A video cassette recorder (VCR) is good investment because it can entertain, educate and exercise you. Tape television programs that will be missed while staying the night in the hospital. Borrow biomedical tapes from the library to spend an easy evening learning. Work out at home anytime with exercise tapes.

Computer knowledge is essential and is the most important career skill I've acquired after my neurosurgical expertise. In my opinion it is underutilized as a tool by doctors. I learned computing in a friendly supportive environment, outside medicine, that became a powerful equalizing weapon against the nonsupporters at the hospital. I am a believer in how much these skills can improve a woman's life. Patient histories are taken from direct questioning right into the word processor. Letters are a snap, the grocery list has a permanent file on the hard disc. This book was written using my personal computer. I track billing with Excel® (Microsoft®) and handle taxes with Quicken® (Microsoft®). I send birthday and Christmas greetings over the internet. I conduct literature searches from home on the internet. It is simply amazing how fast (minutes) an answer to even the most obscure question can be found using the Net, a task which in the good old library days used to take many hours. I have a PC in the office that has access to the World Wide Web. With audio on demand I can listen to the latest news, weather reports, reviews, music, etc. I can read the newspapers from any city, plan my weekend activities or a vacation, scan the medical journals and watch videos all without ever leaving the office. My home computer tracks the schedules and finances of my family. I can import files between the home and the office computers in seconds. I use a lap top computer for remote work when traveling.

E-mail is the most efficient and inexpensive way to keep in touch with busy people in other cities or countries. I receive more e-mail daily than voice mail and it's easier to answer! I have revised articles with a co-worker in another state without ever touching a paper copy using e-mail with attachments and/or file transfer protocol (FTP) between our computers. If these terms sound unfamiliar take a class or invite a computer person to dinner. Become friends with someone who is computer literate and can help get you up to speed. Give it a shot, it is one skill that will place you ahead by saving the most time in the long run. Have fun while doing it!

Stress

Stress has a way of creeping to the surface in the most unflattering ways. It cannot be avoided. Uncover what offsets this feeling and sweeten life with a stash of antidotes that can be summoned from time to time to help make it through. Here are my favorites:

> *I have known my best friend for 30 years. We have this enormous history together and she knows me better than anyone, including myself. Just talking to her, even though we are separated by 6000 miles and several time zones really helps. I feel her concern through the wire and I know in my heart that this woman really cares about me. I am comforted by knowing that I always have someone in my corner who will support me no matter what.*

Appreciate the power of a wonderful girlfriend to neutralize a hellish moment.

Exercise is a good healthy way to unwind and has been a lifelong method for me to relax. I require exercise in my life as much as I need to sleep, but it was often difficult to motivate myself to do any activity after a stressful day in the hospital. Ironically these are the times that one needs to exercise the most. If it requires too much effort to do, it's too easy to talk yourself out of it. During residency I did not have the money or the time to join a gym or health club and if I had, it is unlikely that I would have found the fortitude to make the effort unless it was really convenient.

> *Running has always been my favored activity so in the beginning of residency I would go for a run after sign out rounds, but this became so unpredictable and unpleasant because of safety issues that after the 6 month of internship I abandoned this exercise regimen altogether. I was determined to find another way to fit exercise into my busy schedule.*
>
> *I realized that to remain fit a plan must be designed that was practical to accomplish. I needed to change the way I felt about all those hours spent in the hospital and regard this time as a chance to incorporate some exercise into the rigorous day. I also had to invent a personal exercise routine that could be done at home and save the outside exercising for those rare weekends when a leisurely safe run could be done in good weather and broad daylight.*

Incorporate exercise into the work day. Ponder how many miles are walked during a typical 24 hours of call? Lots. One can gain sufficient exercise while roaming the hospital, but not in the conventional way. Whenever there is an opportunity to climb stairs opt for this over the elevator. This is one tiny but free choice you can make daily that over a long period adds up. Start now and take the stairs to the ICU or wherever for rounds. During my postgraduate fourth year in preparation for my lifelong dream of a Himalayan Mountain trek, I did nothing except take the stairs exclusively for 6 months and it worked to make this vacation one of the most cherished of my entire life. Investigate the onsite equipment including that in the physical therapy department and consider using the machines after hours for a work out or during open time while on call.

Arrange an exercise studio at home. The secret to success with a home exercise program is to have options. Investing in just one type of exercise device will lead to boredom, eventual failure and waste of money. Build diversity into the home regimen. I bought an exercise bike and would ride it for 20 minutes in the evening while watching TV or a medical video. Just seeing the bike sitting there would 'guilt' me into getting on which seemed to be the biggest hurdle. For variety I used repetitions with a weighted jump rope or popped an exercise video in the VCR. If the building is safe get an intense workout by running up and down the stairs, this can be done day or night in all seasons.

After residency, the time and financial restrictions relax, making it possible to join a gym for off hours workouts. The workout uniform has permanent residence in the trunk of my car so that when a cancellation or change of plan at the hospital occurs I don't get disappointed, I get a work out!

Diet

It takes a lot of energy to resist stopping at the nearest fast food restaurant or deli after work or to order a take-out. It is important not to let your diet deteriorate because of being overworked and tired. After several Haagen-Daz frenzies I owned up and began to seize control of this situation. I put serious planning into meals during my residency years. I borrowed a quick trick from the professional arena (remember the progress notes?) and in order to eliminate writing the same items on a grocery list week after week, I created a master shopping list on my word processor and hung copies of this in the kitchen (see Shopping list). On the list were the staples and normally purchased items. I or a family member would use a highlighter pen to indicate what needed replenishing according to the meal planning for the next month.

Shopping list

Vegetables	Fruits	Carbohydrates	Meats
asparagus	apples	bagels	beef
beans	banana	bread	chicken breast
bell pepper	grapefruit	cake	fish
broccoli	grapes	cookies	hamburger
cabbage	lemon	crackers	hot dogs
carrots	lime	English muffin	turkey
cauliflower	melon	flour	
celery	nectarines	frozen pasta	
corn	oranges	frozen pizza	
endives	peach	pasta	
frozen veg	pears	rice	
garlic	plum	rice cakes	
green onions	prune	waffle	
lettuce	raisin		
onions	tangerines		
potatoes			
tomatoes			

Milk Products	Cans/bottles	Mixes/Boxes	Miscellaneous
cheese	apple sauce	cereal	office snacks
cottage cheese	beans	create a meal	
cream cheese	chicken broth	coffee	
eggs	fruit	juices	
ice cream	grapefruit juice	oatmeal	
margarine	soup	ramen	
milk	spaghetti sauce	salad dressing	
mozzarella	tomato juice	tea	
parmesan	tomato sauce	tuna helper	
sour cream	tuna		
yogurt			

Staples			
Ajax	dish detergent	napkins	sponges
bathroom cleaner	Fantastic	oil	static sheets
birth control	female products	paper towels	sugar
brita filter	flu med	Qtips	toilet paper
Clorox	furniture polish	razors	tooth paste
cloth detergent	gel	scrubber	Tylenol
coffee filter	Kleenex	shaving cream	vinegar
conditioner	Listerine	shampoo	Windex
contact lens	lotion	soap	
dental floss	make-up	soy sauce	
deodorant	Murphy's	spices	

I would often cook double amounts of ingredients and use this for two separate meals that week. For example: cook two pounds of ground beef and put half into a casserole for that evening and use the other half for spaghetti later that weekend. I also cook in steps. I begin a meal by preparing part of it in the morning and complete the cooking at dinnertime or asking my partner or child to finish, that way the preparation time is more evenly distributed. Some of my best recipes and tips for kitchen organization come from the women's magazines that patients give to me; after all, these are written by professional mothers. My family's favorite recipes come from the Campbell cook books. These are simply the fastest recipes to make and they taste great. If you are having a guest for dinner, these recipes are ideal but don't forget to hide the cans.

Cook a large pot of stew, chilli, casserole or any meal that can be divided into several individual dinner portions. I then place these servings in throw-away plastic containers, label and freeze these. For a family, quadruple all recipes prior to freezing. Food prepared in this manner is more economical and healthier than buying a frozen meal, not to mention a snap to heat and serve when you are exhausted. Maintaining a variety of these in the freezer gives one a choice in what to eat that evening. After getting home late from a tough day I would pop one of these 'frozen meals' into the microwave. This works so well that even a child can select one from the freezer and create a dinner.

Even if you don't cook you must have at a minimum a recipe for fried rice and pasta because each of these can look so different depending on what is added. Both of these are great 'sweeper' recipes that can be used to get rid of leftovers. Since fried rice tastes best when the rice has been in the refrigerator a few days, cook it earlier on a day off. Fried rice can be cooked in an infinite assortment of ways: add eggs, frozen or fresh vegetables, shrimps, leftover chicken or meat that was cooked for a previous dish, to change the flavor. Take my recipe and personalize it to your own taste.

Fried rice

4 cups cold cooked rice
2 or more teaspoons as needed of salad oil
1 tablespoon soy sauce
1 tablespoon oyster sauce

Optional:
2 well-beaten eggs
2 chopped green onions
1 cup cooked meat, shredded (chicken, pork or shrimp)
1–3 cloves of garlic
½ cup of chopped celery, lettuce, cabbage, bell pepper, etc.

Rub the rice grains until separated. Heat the oil in a frying pan and pour in the eggs. Create a thin omelet, remove and cut into strips. Add the meat and/or vegetables. As the vegetables are cooked add the rice, stir and heat. Flavor with soy sauce and oyster sauce. Sprinkle in the egg strips and green onions and stir fry 1–2 minutes.

A good pasta dish is easy and fast to make at the last minute. Keep both a frozen and dry assortment of pasta always on hand. Use your imagination to add any leftovers to the prepared sauce mixture and experiment with foods that work.

Planning a small dinner party but have no time for cooking? How about a theme party? Order Chinese food and buy the bowls, chopsticks and tea cups to go along. Same goes for Mexican or Italian. Think of extra props to stamp the evening as yours. For larger dinner parties hire a caterer to cook, serve and wash up. It will look extremely well done, there will be enough time to complete hospital responsibilities and enjoy guests while someone else does all the work. Have the regular cleaning person touch up before the event and return again the morning after for cleanup.

Pregnancy

Pregnancy is one of the most difficult issues to grapple with during medical education. The following forewarns of the perils that pregnancy places on one in a profession not yet prepared to make sufficient accommodation to a basic need of nearly half its members. I am hopeful that there will be clarity on this and that instead of regarding pregnancy as disruptive, it will be not only accepted but expected.

There is no right time in medicine for having a child and as I have watched women go through the cycle of pregnancy, I have noted that there is no standard formula that will guarantee a smooth process either. Having a child while in medical school is logistically easier than during residency but then child-care considerations become paramount later during the least flexible portion of medical training in terms of time and financial limitations. The difficulty of pregnancy in residency can be proportional to the demands of that program, your health and the Chief's willingness to be flexible. Due to preset rotations one pregnancy may impact on every other resident's schedule. The co-residents may resent it or at best remain neutral, leaving you in a difficult and lonely position. There is more latitude for child bearing after training but consider that age may preclude such a wish.

If you intend to have children start planning early by reading the literature published by AMWA and the Association of American Medical Colleges which outlines options, statistics and legal rights and gives advice on pregnancy and childcare. Get your partner involved so that he/she is exposed to the complex-ities women in medicine encounter when contemplating preg-nancy. Speak with women who've done it and gather information. Women are very helpful during these times and will not only be your greatest advocates at the job but perhaps your sole support there. Investigate the maternity policies of the program, the allotment for sick leave and vacation time and the protocol for requesting leave. Explore whether or not such absences need to be made up.

Pregnancy brings uncertainty because you cannot predict how you'll feel or what can be accomplished during this time, so prepare for the worst but expect the best. If you are lucky enough to plan the pregnancy, do it during down time when an unexpected absence is less crucial, such as an elective or during a research rotation. Another approach is to plan a pregnancy for the last 3–6 months of residency, after having already proved oneself, when the work demand may be lighter and medical insurance is still in place. Extend maternity leave by arranging a later start date at the new post-residency position. Be aware that interviewing while in the later months of pregnancy may result in bias as some might view you as 'mom' instead of 'doctor'. Don't forget to plan for clothing changes during pregnancy especially with surgical scrubs.

As soon as the test is positive alert the program chief *early*. Allow the other residents to maintain a degree of choice and control by coming to the table with options. This assures that pregnancy will have negligible consequences on your colleagues and they are less likely to resent your situation if they don't have to take on a lot of extra duties. Show the other residents that you want to cooperate fully with the 'team' to minimize any potential changes. Present creative solutions such as doing all clinic or scut work in exchange for being off call during the last months of pregnancy. Cover areas that other residents are less enthusiastic about. Do as many calls as possible early in the pregnancy to make up work ahead of time that will be missed as the pregnancy progresses. Stay home during the day and come to the hospital for overnight call thereby freeing the other residents' nights. Share the work part-time with another resident. Consider combining maternity leave, sick time and vacation time together in the eventuality of an extended absence. If you are forced to cut back, colleagues may grumble if they have to work harder but it's ultimately up to the chief to solve this manpower change.

Hopefully you will have an excellent pregnancy and will be able to carry straight through without blinking an eye, taking maternity leave after delivery. However, if it is a difficult or problematic pregnancy, bedrest may be ordered requiring you to drop all professional duties for many months. Even if you have to take the year off away from the medical scene, continue to keep up-to-date in the field; study for boards, write research papers, organize the home for the new arrival, plan childcare, interview caretakers, continue to monitor billing, do patient follow-ups by phone, etc.

Be aware that pregnancy may inconvenience others no matter when it occurs or how well it's planned, but if this is your wish then health should come first and annoying others is a price that has to be accepted. There is greater ability to call the shots as an attending so have a lawyer write a pregnancy clause in the hiring contract – that way associates will be clear up front that this is a possibility.

Childcare

All working mothers must tackle the childcare dilemma and decide what works for her family. Speak with the other working women about how to handle this. Family may be a preference for assisting in childcare but if that is not feasible, other alternatives will have to be sought. Check out the childcare facilities at the hospital and near home. Consider a babysitter or even a live-in caretaker. That leads to a whole stack of considerations but if your work schedule is unpredictable and includes nights and weekends think about a live-in nanny. Treat this person as an equal partner. Work to solidify and deepen the relationship with this caregiver who will be essential to the well-being of the children. She may even be able to do some housework and cooking. Build up a network of others who may be able to help out in an emergency if, for example, the nanny quits or the baby-sitter doesn't show up for work. Find a pediatrician at your medical center.

Hired help

The greater the financial solidity, the more liberty you have to hire solutions. Revise your thinking and stop doing everything alone.

I don't function effectively in an environment where chaos rules and with the frantic schedule of residency I couldn't carry on with the housework all the time. Besides, I refused to grant the bathrooms or laundry priority over family and friends. During residency I paid a person to clean the apartment and do the laundry every other week which was all I could afford at the time. I didn't want to spend time off dusting, scrubbing or ironing and I still don't. Pay someone to do the domestic work and save the free time for those things that will make you happy. With a family, a cleaning person may need to come more than once per week. Any other errands that have to be done such as shopping for groceries, taking care of the car, mailing letters, dropping off laundry, etc. can be done by hired help. There are also people who will cook meals for the whole week at one setting and freeze these for eating later. Remember you will be, or already are, in a financial position to pay people to make life easier at home, so go for it.

Family: the power to put all into perspective

You may come to a stage professionally when all that you have coveted is finally in reach only to be sidelined because a member of the family needs you more. Later it may be possible to reclaim what has been put on hold in your career or it may be totally lost in the choosing of priorities that distinguish women's lives from men's. Whether it's raising children, concentrating on marriage or taking care of an ill parent or sibling, I believe that children and family will impart a level of immortal satisfaction that over the long run can never be matched by a career, no matter how successful it is. We are not like some of our male counterparts who have the ability to insulate themselves within great careers, and for them this may be enough. For some women, life with a singular focus on career without relinquishing time to the ones we live with may leave a feeling of hollowness, despite professional success.

'Having it all' is a fantasy ideal that exhausts me just trying to imagine it. I'm not in this league. I confess that I have had to make some serious choices about the dreams of womanhood in the pursuit of professional goals. When it comes to choices, listen to those feminine voices that have always guided women and invest time in areas that make you smile the most. Carry on the best you can, doing all that you can, but order priorities, guard those choices and don't regret it. Priorities change as we walk the female life cycle, so pace yourself. Don't judge your career by male standards; instead gauge success within the overall framework of your life.

This whole book is dedicated to becoming more efficient in life so that there is time to appreciate those good things outside of medicine, like family. Open time while on call is a good opportunity to catch up on family and friends by sending letters or phoning. I kept a box of pre-stamped stationary at work in my locker. A note sent by fax or e-mail is an inexpensive and time-saving way of letting someone know they are thought of. I rarely miss a special day or birthday for a loved one because of my master birthday and Christmas gift list. Birthday cards are purchased for the entire year in one stop and mailed out when the appropriate date arrives. Shopping for Christmas and birthday gifts all year around, especially during vacations to exotic places, relieves the pressure of the holidays. Christmas shopping is completed about 6 months ahead of time so that more time can be spent with family. Instead of having to remember the birth date of each niece, nephew or in-law, simply mail gifts for everyone in that family on your brother's or sister's birthday.

Do double duty while on call, hold the beeper and fort down but also carry on with personal 'must dos' like laundry, groceries, repairs, etc. Try to complete the necessities of life during on call time so that during breaks your time can be devoted to family and not consumed by routine errands. During weekend call continue on with life but be prepared for interruptions with a possible trip to the hospital. Start weekend call with a full tank of petrol in the car to avoid wasting minutes at a gas station, especially in the middle of the night in the event that an appearance at the hospital is required. Dress in a professional manner while out and about in case a patient needs to see you. The key to having the ability to be on call and retaining mobility at the same time is the beeper and mobile phone. It's essential to have a cell phone because looking for a pay phone at an unfamiliar place can squander a lot of time. Also helpful is a phone card with access numbers, in case the cell phone fails. At least pages can be answered without the agony of carting a load of quarters. Make use of time waiting in line by placing calls, checking voice mail and doing other business.

Go to performances, concerts and the movies while on call but sit in an aisle seat to facilitate an easy exit if beeped. Discuss special evening plans with the support staff ahead of time with directions to be contacted for urgent matters only. Therefore if paged assume it is important and prepare to leave.

7 The consultants: experts you pay to make post-residency life lucrative

Residency is a finite period of time which most of us somehow get through and move on to the real world. Just as honors in medical school was not a prerequisite for top performance during residency, a successful residency doesn't always translate to a thriving medical career. Likewise a resident who is perceived as weak is not guaranteed to fail later in practice. Because the variables of business enter the game, the distinction between being a resident and being an attending can be vast. Practice involves a variety of skills, some of which were not taught during those many years of training. In practice, the art of medicine becomes the politics and business of medicine.

Type of practice

Investigate what career options exist well before finishing training. There are an infinite variety of practice opportunities depending on specialty, lifestyle and financial goals, such as solo or group private practice, academics, research, government or administration. Consult with attendings and find out what their practices entail.

It may take a while to realize this but as an attending there is more control to incorporate your goals and values together into life and career. In practice you have the ability to pick co-workers and so strengthen the chance of success by going where you are wanted and liked. Select a boss, chief, partner or staff member who is interested in supporting your success. First impressions generally ring true and I have come to heed these signs.

> *From the first minute of the interview many years ago when I met my neurosurgical mentor, I wanted to work with him because here was a neurosurgeon who I liked as a person. He turned out to be the formidable surgeon and teacher that his reputation spoke of, as well as the great person and friend I sensed he would be. On the other hand, whenever I have ignored gut feelings and instead talked myself into thinking that I would be able to work well with a person, I have been sorely wrong.*

If the chemistry is not positive at the onset the probability of fixing it is nil and no amount of money will make it right.

Paying off those loans: salary

Consult with senior residents who are job hunting and begin to gather information about practice early. Investigate what someone at the appropriate level might expect to get paid. Men are generally forthcoming when talking about money if it's not too specific or personal, so ask. A professional way of inquiring about this is to phrase the question this way 'How much would a person at my level expect to be paid?' or 'What is the salary range of a person with my or your qualifications?' Get clear on the salary numbers and decide what is acceptable prior to beginning any job discussion. Request an amount that is about 20–30% higher than what you will actually agree to thereby securing the targeted salary after negotiations. Women tend to undervalue themselves when it comes to money so never answer a question like 'How much would you like to be paid?' from a potential boss without doing research first. This is a ploy employers use to secure a bargain for themselves. Instead turn the question on them and ask what your predecessor was paid.

Contract

Research the benefits package including secretarial support (it's better not to share a secretary with a male colleague), parking space, service/emergency number and beeper, cell phone, office size, voice mail, educational leave, maternity leave, call schedule, billing arrangements, insurance applications, provider numbers, incentive pay, etc. Get admitting privileges at all institutes in the practice group, or academic center, full or part time. Discuss any expected administrative duties and termination clauses. A good way to discover the rigors of 'call' is to examine the printout of phone calls that the service handles at nights and weekends.

After deciding upon the practice situation get it in writing. A contract adds clarity to the relationship and allows all parties to understand the parameters of operation. The clearer the rules are initially, the better chance of avoiding conflict, misunderstanding and stress in the future. Personal considerations or other reasons often cause women to think that they are not in a strong position to bargain during contract negotiations. Hire a consultant for advice during this process in order to obtain the best arrangement. These consultants, usually lawyers, are worth the fee especially if you are inexperienced and naive about contracts. Make it clear with this consultant that what is needed is assistance with the actual negotiation of the contract and not just a review of the final agreement. Ask the consultant the best way to alert the new colleagues that there will be someone present on your behalf at the negotiation table. Placing a third party between you and your new colleagues removes you from the nitty gritty of negotiating with them but remember to maintain a position of mutual respect as these are your future associates.

Schedule periodic review sessions with the boss to allow adequate time to make adjustments and review performance. Even after commencing the job continue to compare arrangements with those of colleagues at your level regarding pay and benefits. After attaining a stronger bargaining position, persevere in upgrading the contract yearly.

Career goals

As residency was ending and I was about to undertake my own practice, I established the following career goals: continue to grow as a surgeon technically as well as passing specialty boards, develop a productive practice by marketing myself while at the same time learning the business of medicine, improve my personal financial portfolio by consulting with an adviser and minimize the risk of a law suit.

The business

The closer the philosophies of business and life the better the chance of being successful in both. Merge personal values and goals with those of the profession. After being an attending for a while I learnt that there are important entities that cannot be sacrificed, even for a fat paycheck. Retain a genuine bedside presence but develop a firm/strong business approach to your practice. Learn about your overheads.

Control access people have to you by limiting those who can page you directly. Always be available to patients and medical personnel but place a filter between you and the medical world by giving out the office number only. This allows the selection of what to answer and what to delegate. Early in my attending career I mistakenly gave out the beeper number to a wide variety of medical staff who further gave it to others, including patients.

> *I remember being paged on Thanksgiving Day in the middle of the feast by a patient's daughter of whom I was a peripheral consultant and over a nonurgent question that should have been handled by the attending physician of record.*

If your beeper number is known, people will use it and often overstep normal protocol even when there are trained staff in place to manage these questions.

In my first attending position I sensed that people often felt that I was more 'approachable' than my male associate and were not hesitant to call me for issues that should have been handled at a less senior level, or should even have been taken by the male associate. Even though you have a different style than other colleagues don't get into the trap of taking on their work. Firmly remind clerks, nurses, technicians and other physicians who to call and refuse to do work which is another's responsibility. If it's not your business gently direct the person the right way.

Have business cards printed prior to starting a new position so that these can be passed out during introductions. After the name, the second largest print should be the phone number. Too often I am handed business cards that practically require a magnifying glass to see the office phone number. Look at a variety of business cards and select one that is impressive and smartly designed. On the card include fax number and e-mail as a growing number of professionals are communicating this way.

The first item to check in the morning is the office voice mail. I use voice mail communication to sign off to colleagues and they in turn leave messages overnight or when I'm in the operating room. If you've been up all night on call and have to change office plans for the morning, give the staff instructions by leaving a voice mail message for the office. That way, the office personnel can carry on in the morning while you catch up on sleep. My biller and I communicate almost exclusively via voice mail. Voice mail is becoming so common that even patients are no longer surprised to hear a machine answering in the office. First time patients usually want to speak to a person but after they have met you they become comfortable with leaving messages if trust has been established. Voice mail is more economical for routine matters than an answering service.

Billing is not discussed much during residency and I didn't know the difference between Medicare and Medicaid when I opened practice but I sure learned fast. Flip through the Current Procedural Terminology (CPT) code book and the International Classification of Diseases Clinical Modification (ICDCM) reference. These codes are crucial to processing an insurance claim and getting paid. Spend a few hours assisting an attending in the office. Note the office layout, observe the billers, scan patient sign-in forms and billing forms. Thumb through a few charts to see how these are organized and observe follow-up protocols. I've learnt most about the 'business' of medicine by flipping through the charts of established physicians. Monitor those who do the billing, not only for theft but for lack of motivation. I prefer that my billing be done off premises by professional billers so that the immediate office personnel is not privy to monetary information. While between billers I actually did it for 3 months until a replacement was hired. It was a great learning experience and allowed me to understand and track the future billing better. Learn from the professionals and enroll in a course on billing or hire a consultant for advice on increasing the efficiency of the office. Establish a relationship with an accountant to monitor the office accounts.

Although my practice philosophy could fill another book, here are just a few of the important techniques out of many that have helped to develop a following. Just acquiring patients is a formidable task because of politics and the old boy network. In most specialties, patients are the currency and physicians must compete for this pool. Hone your skills and talents to break the cycle of physicians referring to men only, leaving women out of the pot. At first I was amazed over the type of referrals from certain physicians: difficult patients (one exposed his concealed loaded handgun during the examination), litigious people, patients who had a history of nonpayment or those that another physician just wanted to be rid of with pathology unconnected to my specialty. It was puzzling that these same physicians would make appropriate referrals to the male associates. After demonstrating my willingness to serve challenging patients some of these referring doctors became my strongest allies and a secure referral base for desirable patients. Other attendings ignored this, keeping to the same pattern of referral by sending only these types of patients to my office and the more suitable ones to my male associate. After a few years of this pattern I decided that this was a one-way game that was disruptive to my practice so I stopped

68

accepting their patients except for emergencies. Nurture the referral base by prompt follow-up and communication but do not allow double-standard treatment by a referring physician, male or female. The best advertisements are the patients who will themselves refer cases and also return to their primary physician with compliments about you.

Communicate like a man to colleagues but listen like a woman to patients

The dominant culture in medicine is male, and women must learn to navigate these waters by looking at the world from a man's perspective. At the same time she must resist becoming a male clone, staying true to her feminine self in order to remain a woman. You will be happier and your practice will thrive if you just be yourself. Some of the most bitter women are those who succumbed to being 'one of the boys'. Use your female talents to build the practice because these are the very qualities that will attract and keep patients. Women have the capacity to practice medicine in a style that is a departure from the traditional male way. The public is hungry for this option. The feminine touch brings an alternative approach to the practice of medicine and there are patients who prefer this style.

Listening is at the forefront of my medical practice philosophy. Some men are not great listeners and others simply don't value listening, but patients do. Patients feel more relaxed and open around women physicians. They will therefore want to talk more and will expect a woman doctor to listen. They may be intimidated by a male physician or they may unconsciously feel that a woman's time is not as valuable as a man's. The reasons don't matter because the dividends for investing the extra time and listening are worth it. I am surprised at the compliments when all I've done for a 30 minute consultation is listen. The patient often says 'This is the best doctor I've ever talked with' and all I contributed was my ear! I expend more time listening and interacting with my patients than the male surgeons but also spend less time trying to fix a misunderstanding caused by poor communication. An extra 30 minutes of conversation with a patient or their family goes a long way towards establishing a favorable relationship. I listen to my patients because (a) I often learn important information related to their medical condition that might otherwise never be uncovered, and (b) I would rather give them an hour of my time at the start, than months in court down the line. By listening to a patient you validate their value as a person and demonstrate character. Not only are patients more likely to do better if they sincerely feel you care about them but they are also less apt to sue. Build a stable of patients who believe in you, it makes business pleasant and the bill will be paid.

Effective listening doesn't mean letting a patient commandeer the appointment or consultation with meaningless ramble. It is gently but firmly leading the patient in a direction in which the doctor can acquire medically relevant facts while at the same time the patient feels that he/she has had an unrushed and genuine opportunity to express their feelings and often *fears*. Give this patient the chance to do so but maintain control. Develop closure phrases to politely signal an end to the exam, such as 'One more question before I leave' or 'Before we end....'. Another method is to identify the time parameters prior to beginning, 'I have 20 minutes to exam you, so let's get started right away'.

Further tips for success

❑ Look clean and well-groomed in the professional setting.

❑ Demonstrate meticulous standards by washing your hands in front of the patient before starting the exam. They always notice.

❑ When an unexpected urgent matter surfaces, send staff in to warn the patient that the doctor has an emergency. Don't rush the patient without alerting them of the circumstances first. Give this patient full attention even though an exam may have to be shortened and they will need to return for a more thorough visit.

❏ Don't offhandedly complain to the patient about being tired and don't look exhausted either.

❏ When a patient calls, come to the phone or return the call personally as often as possible. If I am in the operating room I often make my phone calls to patients' homes in the evening and the patients are gratefully surprised. Who wouldn't feel good to know that their doctor is thinking about them even at that hour.

❏ Families never mind being contacted and awoken in the middle of the night regarding a loved one.

❏ Patients or their families can better accept bad news if it is told to them first by the doctor and they don't discover it for themselves or learn about it by accident through another source.

❏ Be wary of staff who may transmit conflicting information to the patient. Instruct staff to begin a patient's questions with 'What did Dr Attending say about that?' That way everyone is consistently speaking the same message and the team has the appearance of cohesion.

❏ Encourage an unsure or difficult patient to go for a second opinion.

❏ Never discuss money with a patient unless they bring it up first. This is what the staff should be trained to do. Give patients the impression that the main concern is them and not the bill. Take the high road when it comes to money and the patient.

❏ Watch out about playing with too much technology, especially in the ICU setting which can leave the person out altogether. I can turn on the technology when necessary but I never forget the human behind the machines and laboratory values.

In the hospital or organization get to know the administration; they have the power to neutralize a hostile colleague and to furnish additional advantages if you are worth it to them. These people are very sensitive to the bottom line numbers, something your clinical chief may not be as savvy about. Think of these people as an additional pool of allies especially if you have performed well as a rainmaker.

Malpractice

During training, residents are rather insulated about medical–legal threats but these issues will pervade your practice. If called to court during residency go, because it may be the only occasion to be in a courtroom as a minor player and therefore observer of the proceedings. If sued later the courtroom won't look as daunting. The first 3 months after my residency were devoted to learning about malpractice. Get expert consultant advice in this domain by reading books and taking courses. One line of advice: be sincere and treat the patients like gold. If unable to, or your intuition about this person is worrisome, then send the patient to another physician. The most delicate judgment to master in medicine is when to pass on a patient and let someone else manage the case. There is always another doctor willing to take on the responsibility and if your instincts say 'No' then pass.

Be wary of requests for medical advice in hallways or at parties. I have often been sought out at social events with questions of a medical nature. I answer in this manner 'I would like to discuss this with you but I can not give you the attention you deserve right now, why not call the office and make an appointment?' Not a single person out of many has ever followed this up with a call – it seems as though they just wanted free advice.

Personal $

After the educational loans are paid off, begin to accrue financial clout. Find a consultant who can honestly design a financial plan. Don't try to manage this alone, go to the experts to make the most of earnings. After going to several seminars regarding personal finances, I attended a focused AMWA meeting and met the consultant who has advised me. Within 6 months of leaving residency, a financial plan was hatched which included disability insurance, investments and retirement. Get a recommendation from another professional and speak with several financial advisers before purchasing anything.

8 Her way

Ann: on balance

Ann had longed to be an obstetrician since the age of 8 but finances necessitated a change in plans so she decided on nursing school instead. She practiced nursing for 6 years where she met two wonderful physician mentors through whom her original dream of medical school resurfaced. While working full time, Nurse Ann financed her pre-medical education and on the third attempt at age 30 was accepted into a Caribbean-based medical school.

These same loyal mentors continued to cheer Ann on, one even invited her to be a visiting medical student at his prestigious New England Institute. This mentor assisted Ann in extending the clerkship into a year long stay which led to her acceptance into a competitive residency. After completing obstetrics and gynecology training, Dr Ann became an attending at a major inner city academic medical center. She over-compensated for her foreign medical diploma by working ultra long hours. She devoted herself to the job and was hailed as having built a strong gynecology service. One of her mottos during this time was 'Gee, isn't this good that I'm not married and don't have kids because that way I can work even harder.'

On the eve of her fiftieth birthday, she is settled into a less demanding position at a prestigious and glamorous hospital. She now has time to ponder her opportunities both taken and lost and to reflect on life as a single woman.

Tips and advice

❑ Remember the support of your mentors. Remain in contact and recognize the contribution of supporters to your career as it develops.

❑ During discussions, the points should be clear and concise. When conferring on a topic keep the dialog to a minimum.

❑ It is important to cultivate a professional relationship with the nurses. Be pleasant but firm. This is advice from an ex-nurse.

❑ Look professional. Maintain good grooming by having well-kept hair, nails, make-up and dress.

❑ Sexism is still present but less so than before.

❑ Keep your personal life private. Stifle the urge to discuss personal matters with those at work, the less others know the better. Don't open confidences until you have judged if this person can be trusted. It takes time to know who is and isn't trustworthy.

❑ Avoid on-the-job affairs if possible or be very discrete if you must. Co-workers will learn of the affair sooner or later because there is no way to really keep this type of activity private, no matter how careful the two of you are.

❑ Confusing the job with life will leave you feeling a void. Invest more time in yourself and have a life outside of medicine. Learn to balance time between the hospital and your non-medical activities. Don't fool yourself into thinking that the job can fulfill all your personal needs.

❑ Don't make the career your sole goal. There is such a situation as being a professional success but a personal failure. Attend to those feminine needs and develop well-thought-out personal goals as well. Balance both your personal and professional lives.

Experiences

Ann reported to her pre-med advisor that she had just received the first medical school rejection. The pre-med advisor then told her to stop wasting time because 'You are never going to get into medical school'. Ann ran out of the woman's office in tears and was leaving through the revolving doors when at that same instant she noticed Dr S entering the building. Ann had worked as a recovery room nurse with some of Dr S's patients and had known him for over 4 years. Dr S spotted Ann, pulled her out of the doorway and asked what was wrong. After the explanation, he surprisingly said 'My wife is a pre-med advisor, come with me'. In a span of a minute one door closed and another opened. She walked into the office and began a supportive relationship with a new advisor that spanned 2 years.

After her second rejection Ann felt like quitting but the new advisor and Dr S refused to hear of it and urged her to continue. On the next and third try she got accepted to medical school.

> *Moral: Even in the dimmest situation you will find true allies. Shed those who are not interested in helping you and stick to those who truly care.*

While working as an attending, Ann applied for a competitive fellowship at her institution and for 2 years in a row was turned down. Ann wanted this career path so dearly that she overlooked early warning statements like 'Even though you're a woman we'd consider you...' or 'We took a man this year...'. She worked very hard in her job to prove her worth, sacrificing all balance to do so. In fact the whole reason for remaining in the currently held position was in the hopes of gaining that coveted fellowship.

On her third try she was judged to be a 'sure thing' for this fellowship by her colleagues. She was virtually 'promised' the position. The fellowship director and her current Chief made numerous statements to her and her coworkers beginning with 'When Ann is the fellow...'. At a departmental conference he even announced that Ann would soon be leaving to begin this fellowship. She confronted her Chief afterward and reminded him that she had not even had her interview yet. He dismissed this by explaining that in her case the interview was for courtesy only and that 'We all know you're going to get it anyway'.

The 'courtesy' interview came and ended in a disaster. The Director of the fellowship began to lay the ground work for what Ann realized was going to be the third rejection. She told Ann that they had reservations about her skills, etc. Ann left the interview knowing that she was beaten by a male resident 5 years junior to her experience level. In the taxi home she erupted into tears.

> *Moral: Don't sacrifice everything to chase an unattainable goal. If the deck is stacked against you from the beginning a lot of time and energy will be wasted trying unsuccessfully to change it. Give it your best shot then move on and never forget that unless it is in writing, it doesn't exist.*

Fiona: the big trade-off paid off

Fiona was always in a rush. She finished high school at 16, graduated college at 20, became a wife at 21, a medical doctor at 24 and a mother at 25. She was one of 10 women in a class of 150 medical students to graduate in 1963. She married a future nephrologist, completed a pediatrics residency and then embarked on 20 years of part-time pediatric clinic work (3 days/week) while raising four children. Now with her youngest in college, she has settled into a challenging position as the Chairperson of Pediatrics and Acting Director of Ambulatory Care at the community hospital in her neighborhood. Instead of working part-time she is now doing double duty and loves it.

Tips and advice

❑   Keep some time for yourself aside from that invested in family and job.

❑   Work for a boss who will judge your performance by its merits, not on superfluous talents like how well a game of golf is played or the type of car driven.

❑   If you are planning to have kids, you will probably have to negotiate a career trade off. Even with the best husband and child caregiver, it will be difficult to devote as much time to the career as is needed to advance up the success ladder in the same timeframe as a male counterpart. When the children are young, it may be necessary to put your career on temporary hold. Although Fiona worked part-time for 20 years so that she was able to devote time to the children, she is comfortable with this decision and feels it was worth it. She is proud of having raised children who are 'great people' and believes that it is possible to catch up on most career goals after the personal ones are satisfied.

❑   Develop a relationship with a caregiver in which she is your partner. Her caregiver remained with the family for 18 years, which provided a substantial source of stability for the children.

Experiences

The year was 1964 and Fiona was an intern in pediatrics on a medicine rotation when she learned she was 3 months pregnant. She was directed by her chief resident, a woman, to the Chairman of Internal Medicine with the caution that 'He may very well throw you out!'. This particular Chairman, a bachelor, was an imposing, authoritative, strict, respected academician of the 'old world'. After steeling herself but still shaking, she rode the elevator to the penthouse of the chairman's building, terrified of what she imagined would come. She was led into a humongous office/palace with this famous man sitting behind a giant polished desk/throne. She blurted out the news, expecting disaster.

Without pause he said 'Congratulations, I am sure you will work it out'. She couldn't believe what she heard, it was that simple. All the hype and terror were unfounded and she literally skipped out of the office on to completing both internship and an excellent pregnancy.

> *Moral: Expect the best in spite of the unknown.*

With her children in school, Fiona decided to expand to full-time and accepted a job as the Director of Ambulatory Pediatrics in a community hospital under Dr R, the Chief of the Pediatric Service. Dr R had a horrible history of being impossible to work with and colleagues alerted Fiona of his reputation. Because her career up to this point had been positive, she disregarded these warnings and took the job believing it inconceivable that his personality could be that destructive to her work effort.

Although she worked hard and was appreciated by her colleagues, Dr R never gave her much credit for these efforts and at times claimed positive results as his own. He demanded total control over all staff members in the department and even had a manager who was known to act as his 'spy' reporting on the petty daily doings in the office. Fiona was told by the 'spy' that she had been seen eating lunch with people from other departments and it was preferred by Dr R that all staff members lunch only at the 'pediatric table'.

After Fiona successfully organized and carried out a city wide conference, he became even more obstructive and vindictive. The Christmas party for that year was planned at an expensive restaurant. Dr R ordered Fiona to remain behind to oversee the hospital activities while all of the senior and junior staff were elegantly dined. He repeatedly refused her requests for vacation time. He often reassigned the doctors from her area without consulting with Fiona first. This meant that the physician/patient balance was upset and Fiona would often have to work through her lunch time to ensure that patient care was not compromised. In short, over a two year course he made her life in that department miserable and confirmed that he was as bad as his reputation.

Despite his maneuvering she continued to be well-liked by both the patients and the other medical staff. He got so jealous of Fiona's success that finally he asked her to resign telling her she was overqualified for the job. She began to physically suffer and finally confided in a trusted colleague who had been aware of Dr R's behavior to Fiona and others. The colleague advised 'I'm not saying that you are not right and that you wouldn't make a better chief but I advise you to go because you will not be successful in unseating him'. She contacted a lawyer to review her rights and he assured Fiona that her performance and professionalism would not be challenged. More importantly he advised that the decision to continue working was hers and not Dr R's. In the midst of this, a position suddenly opened at another institute so she was able to leave on her terms to a chief level job in a more supportive environment.

> *Moral: There will be times when you win the popular vote but lose the battle politically. Don't wait too long in taking steps to minimize the damage to yourself, emotionally, spiritually, morally and physically. Fear not exiting an untenable situation.*

Lisa: a niche is nice

Lisa's first diploma was a Master's degree in home economics and her next degree at age 30 was a medical doctorate, class of 1980. After braving a residency in urology she went into solo private practice where training in the business of medicine was begun. Lisa taught herself the finer points and forged a thriving practice.

In the process of survival she discovered a niche designed around women that is now her entire practice.

Now in her mid forties, this single, world-traveler is very happy with her life. Lisa enjoys a wide variety of social events and involvement with the local AMWA chapter.

Tips and advice

☐ Your success is not a result of luck, you are there because you are good. Often women think that somehow they got a break and reached their status because of luck. Men on the other hand know that success is related to their talent.

☐ Take courses on the business of medicine. Look for seminars at the State Medical Society for assistance in administering your practice.

☐ Those in private practice need to monitor the financial changes in medicine. As a guard against any future economic down-turns, continue to educate yourself and stay up with the trends facing medicine.

☐ Sending those claims to collection? Send to collection only those claims that patients have received from their insurance companies. Trying to collect on claims from patients who simply haven't paid will be largely a frustrating waste of time and the patient may become antagonistic.

Experiences

When Lisa opened up her office she figured that she would be able to successfully compete with male colleagues for the common variety of patients. She anticipated encountering the normal mix of cases typical in this field but the expected referrals didn't come in the volume required to sustain practice. After a while, Lisa realized that these types of patients were never going to be referred and no amount of forcing would change this. It was simply the reality of being a woman in the male-dominated and male-oriented specialty of urology.

What impressed Lisa was that she was receiving consultations but not the predictable type – instead her office was full of women. Her referrals were women patients that male urologists were not particularly interested in seeing. It dawned on her that here was a huge need that was not being met. She hatched a plan not only to accept these patients but to welcome them and build a lucrative practice around this niche.

If your practice is not developing, reverse this trend by exploiting a niche in which others will not be able to successfully compete against you. Examine the type of patients that come to the office, these are generally sent for a reason. Study your particular strengths and match these to those referrals. Use creativity in building a practice out of what comes to you naturally instead of wasting time trying to chase cases that go elsewhere.

> *Moral: Your practice may be different from others in the specialty but what you make of this difference will determine your success.*

Patient Q, the last patient of a long day, was a referral to Lisa from another urologist (red flag). Patient Q had a pyschiatric history and was obviously in the throes of a psychotic episode at the time of her visit to Lisa's office. Lisa immediately understood the patient's psychiatric situation and after a physical exam concluded that Patient Q was in the wrong specialist's office. Lisa ended the exam by contacting the patient's psychiatrist after which the patient became upset and firmly refused to leave the office. Finally after about an hour of pleading and cajoling, a member of Lisa's staff was able to put Patient Q in a taxi. The patient later responded with hostile phone calls and letters but was not given a follow-up appointment and eventually got treatment with the appropriate professional, elsewhere.

Every now and then patients are seen or referred who for whatever reason, whether they are unstable, abusive, difficult, etc., the doctor may not wish to continue a professional relationship with. Minimize your exposure in these cases by limiting the visit to a physical exam to rule out life-threatening pathology and better yet, instead just listen. Don't encourage the patient–doctor relationship by initiating non-urgent tests, procedures or instrumentation. After an intrusion of this sort has commenced with such a patient, they will consider you his/her doctor and termination of the relationship once it has progressed beyond this stage is more troublesome.

> *Moral: If you feel that a particular patient will not fit into your practice, politely end the relationship as early as possible.*

Shay: long journey out

When her mother discovered her at age 5 dissecting a doll and then later a frog, it was apparent to Shay's family that she would be a doctor. It was not so obvious to the family that she also began to realize around this time that she was a lesbian. That truth would have to wait decades for a formal announcement. So she spent the balance of her life pursuing the first dream and stifling the other reality trying to 'do what was expected of a woman at that time growing up in Texas', and she did this very well.

Shay became one woman among 75 students to graduate from medical school, class of 1962. Shay married and delivered son number one during the second year of medical school and son number two at the end of her senior year despite 9 straight months of the worst morning sickness. She beat her future mentor (Dr H) and his surgical residents at golf while 6 months pregnant, after which Dr H came to be Shay's loudest sponsor.

Under Dr H's guidance, she began an internship in preparation for a career in pediatric surgery with two infant sons at home. Two months into the program she looked around at the only other role models, guys who had sacrificed everything personally, and had second thoughts. The program was seven more years at this intensity so she made a painful decision and said 'yes' to her kids and 'no' to a career in surgery. She felt as though she had jumped ship and was letting her avid supporter, Dr H, down. Shay imagined that he had held this opinion of her 'You see this woman pediatric surgeon, she's tough and I put her there over a man'. She told him that she was unwilling to sacrifice family in the pursuit of a career in pediatric surgery. All he said when she broke the news to him was 'So don't do it'.

Meanwhile after stifling a beloved career dream for the sake of her kids she was able to find satisfaction as an academic pediatrician, for a while. It gnawed on her through the years until finally at age 47 with the youngest son in college, she took stock of herself. She quit the prestigious professor job and returned to do a residency in emergency medicine, and came out as a lesbian.

Tips and advice

- ☐ Power speaks and rules. If you intend to make a major difference you must maneuver into a position of power but be prepared to make a lot of personal sacrifices.

- ☐ Doctors who smile more get sued less.

- ☐ Patients need to hear things twice. Repeat important instructions often to a patient and preferably to a family member also.

- ☐ When someone mistakenly calls you nurse, reply by saying 'That's the nicest compliment I've heard all day but I'm actually your doctor'.

- ☐ If the patient needs something, get it. If the appropriate staff is not available to assist the patient, do it for the patient's sake. He/she will greatly appreciate it.

- ☐ The raising of children is more important than the actual birthing. Devote the necessary time to the rearing of your children.

- ❑ A live-in caretaker is essential when the children are below school age.

- ❑ An academic career is more conducive to family life. Often the hours in an academic position are more flexible and therefore better controlled by you.

Experiences

Shay's last rotation in medical school was as an honor student in surgery while pregnant. It was expected that the students would have pre-rounded on each patient prior to formal rounds with the attendings and entire resident staff. On this particular morning she was late getting to the hospital because her infant son was sick at home. She had not been able to pre-round and didn't even have time to look up the patient's vital signs. Naturally the first patient for formal rounds was hers and she realized that she would have to wing it. She made her presentation with the patient's history which included several complications and a secondary infection. Then she concluded by saying 'Mrs Patient I see that you are doing much better this morning' to which the patient replied 'oh yes I am'. At this stage Dr H interjects and asks 'Mrs Patient, how are you *really* doing?' Mrs Patient again replied 'Much better.' Dr H then turned to Shay in front of the team and asked 'Now how did you know that she was finally better?' When Shay replied, 'She's got her make-up on and her hair set', Dr H was so impressed that he announced to the entire floor 'That answer alone makes me want more women in medicine'.

> *Moral: A woman doctor may appreciate characteristics or changes in a patient that a male physician might overlook. Use your female instincts and allow yourself to deliver the best care to your patients by seeing beyond the lab values and numbers.*

During a psychiatric rotation in medical school Shay stood before the class presenting a case of a patient with ulcerative colitis in perfectly noticeable Texan twang. 'This here 14-year-old boy got chronic da-rear...'. The professor frowned and interrupted her at this point saying to the class 'Where did we get this foreigner from?'. Then he continued to the merriment of the other students, 'Young lady we know where it comes from but the word is *diarrhea*'. Shay went aphasic and the class roared. She felt humiliated in front of her classmates and managed to struggle to the end of the presentation before the tears came. At home that night she announced to her husband that she was going to lose the Texas accent at language school; and she did but she hasn't forgotten the imprint that that comment carried.

Moral: Discrimination in any form leaves an underlying edge of sorrow and anger which can affect all that you do. But know that you will survive as Shay did, 62 years and practicing.

9 Discharge instructions

If this book has meant anything to you, pass it on to another woman so that her life and career can be kinder. Inspire the women around you to join forces instead of dissolving into micropockets of jealousy and bitterness that splinter more than bind us. May we support one another because all women benefit in spite of only one or two moving ahead at a time. Find the courage to elevate women even if it means that they will surpass and be better than you. Then imagine your daughter poised on their shoulders as part of an unyielding feminine ladder and know that her life will be higher for it. And have comfort that despite the 1000 nights, 18000 miles and a few sundry tears spent to get here, this woman would chance the journey again.

Acknowledgements

With gratitude to the following who supported and participated in the preparation of this book

Deanna Mukai
Matt Schudel
Gary G. Wong, esq.
Martha Palubniak, M.D.
Brenda Vecchione, P.A.
Ron Erickson, M.S.
Zoya Melnikov, M.S.
Shay Bintliff, M.D.
Suzanne Frye, M.D.
Frances McGill, M.D.
Roseann Caserio
Setareh Sharif, Ph.D.
Phyllis Weiner, M.D.
Eric Michalowski, patient
Nat Russo
 and
Gilbert Romano